UNCHAINED

OUR FAMILY'S ADDICTION MESS
IS OUR MESSAGE

Nancy McCann Vericker
&
JP Vericker

Published by Clear Faith Publishing, LLC
100 Stevens Landing Dr., #206
Marco Island, FL 34145
www.clearfaithpublishing.com

Cover and Interior Design by Doug Cordes

The interior is typeset in Molde and Paperback.

ISBN: 978-1-940414-22-5

DEDICATION

To Joe—You had me at hello.

EPIGRAPH

Blackbird singing in the dead of night,
Take these broken wings and learn to fly.
All your life,
You were only waiting for this moment to arise.

Blackbird singing in the dead of night,
Take these sunken eyes and learn to see.
All your life,
You were only waiting for this moment to be free.

Blackbird fly, blackbird fly
Into the light of the dark black night.

The Beatles
"Blackbird"

CONTENTS

FOREWORD

As a board-certified physician in addiction medicine, I work with families on a daily basis as I treat patients suffering from substance abuse disorders. *Unchained: Our Family's Addiction Mess Is Our Message*, by Nancy Vericker and her son, JP, describes their family's journey from drug addiction to recovery and is a story millions of families can identify with. This book will help families understand that addiction is not a moral failing, but a medical disease with professional treatment options available to help them deal with this harrowing epidemic.

I first met Nancy through her son, JP, whose addiction and recovery story is at the heart of this book. JP is my trusted colleague, a tireless and dedicated professional who has been working in the field of addiction treatment for many years. Oftentimes those who have suffered from substance abuse disorders and were able to recover have chosen to undergo education and training to work in the field of addiction treatment and help others recover. JP is one of those people. He has worked in several professional treatment settings and co-founded Northeast Addictions Treatment Center in Quincy, Massachusetts, a Boston suburb. JP has taught me much about the field of addiction as we have worked closely together at NEATC. Many young and suffering persons have found the professional treatment they need to combat the disease of addiction from his message of hope, based on his own experience with addiction and recovery.

Unchained details the struggles of JP and his family as they battled the disease of addiction in the years before his recovery. Nancy and JP share many of the harmful and painful consequences they suffered from his persistent drug use. Addiction is a chronic, relapsing brain disease that is characterized by compulsive drug use despite harmful consequences. This disease does not discriminate; it affects those across all races, all socioeconomic classes, all geographical locations, and all ages. Untreated addiction is ultimately a fatal illness.

As importantly, addiction is also a family disease, which negatively impacts the physical emotional well-being of all family members, disrupting their relationships. Nancy describes in detail the many people, both recovery professionals and others, who helped her and her loved ones through their family's addiction crisis. Her honest portrayal of her family's generational struggle with addiction and their subsequent recovery together serves as a learning tool for others suffering from addiction.

According to the National Survey on Drug Use and Health (NSDUH), 21.5 million American adults (age 12 and older) suffered from a substance use disorder in 2014. Each year the numbers of Americans affected by drug and alcohol addiction increases. The opioid epidemic was declared a national health emergency on October 26, 2017. The Center for Disease Control reports that in 2016, more than forty-six Americans died every day from overdoses involving prescription opioids.

This disease affects millions and their families, but because of the stigma associated with it, many of these families are reluctant to talk about it and afraid to seek treatment. The message in Nancy and JP's account in *Unchained* is not to be afraid to seek help for the addict and for the family. This book stands as a source of encouragement and hope for families to get treatment and support for the addict and their loved ones to break the stronghold of addiction and enter a life of recovery together.

If you or a loved one is struggling with addiction, reach out for help as soon as possible.

1. Visit Northeast Addictions Treatment Center online at neaddictions.com or call 888-852-4320.

2. The Substance Abuse and Mental Health Services Administration, (SAMHSA) provides a national helpline providing free, confidential, 24/7, 365-day treatment referral and information service (in English and Spanish) for individuals and families suffering from substance use disorders. This service provides referrals to local treatment centers, support groups, and community-based organizations. Call 1-800-662-HELP or visit their online treatment services locator https://findtreatment. samhsa.gov.

3. The National Council on Alcoholism and Drug Dependence (NCADD) website offers three simple tests aimed at determining if an individual has a substance abuse problem. These tests comprise three categories: "Are you wondering if you have an alcohol problem?", "Are you wondering if you have a drug problem?", and "Self-Test for Teenagers." Visit their website at ncadd.org.

4. Twelve Step groups are free and available at the local level at a variety of convenient times and locations. For further information, visit the Alcoholics Anonymous website at aa.org.

5. Family physicians, health care providers and local faith leaders are also a good source of information for guidance in seeking help with addiction issues.

Dr. Amy Fitzpatrick, MS, MD

Medical Director, Northeast Addiction Treatment Center
Board Certified in Internal Medicine and Addiction Medicine

PREFACE

This book was born out of a desire to help families in the fight of their lives, as we were, to free themselves from the stranglehold of addiction. It is told from two points of view: my son's and mine.

Like all accounts of addiction, it is a family story, as it impacted all of us: my husband, our three daughters, our son, and me. It was not an easy decision to go "public" and share the details of one of the most painful chapters of our lives. JP and I chose to do so after being contacted by families who learned of our story of desperation and hope and wanted to know how that could happen for them, too. Our family has been given the gift of a renewed life together. A gift is meant to be shared, and so we decided to share all of it—the gritty and the glorious.

JP gave his account of events in his own words, which I took down interview style over a period of months. Where necessary, names, genders, and titles have been changed to ensure the privacy of others.

ACKNOWLEDGMENTS

Sincere appreciation to Teresa Knipper for opening the door and Jim Knipper of Clear Faith Publishing for believing in this story. Many thanks to Marie Cortissoz Houlihan and Evelyn McCormack for their longtime friendship and for once again cleaning up my prose. Thank you to Kathleen Hollenbeck for her sensitivity to text and attention to detail. Thanks to Father Mark Mossa, SJ, Grace and Brian McLaren, and Rev. Heather Wright, who believed in me as a writer and helped with the nuts and bolts.

Thank you with all my heart to my spiritual director, Sister Kathleen Kuczkowski, OSU, for more than two decades of prayerful listening and guidance, and to Dr. Bill Cipriano for his wisdom. Deepest thanks to my brother-in-law Bob Vericker, my brother, Jim McCann, my sister-in-law Tara Griffin, and Tina Crocitto and her family for their love, straight talk, and laughter over the long haul.

Thank you to my beloved friends for the gift of their presence: Kathy Hannon, Margaret Lewis, James Rohrig, the Hershman family, Eileen Harrington, Ann Lynch, Anne Curran, Barbara and Mark McCarthy, Catherine Bradley, Mary Lou Brusco, Val Sprague, Gail Obenour, and Bebbie Chickering.

Thank you to Taylor D'Ottavio and Ellen McCarthy for reading the manuscript.

Thank you to all who shared their experience, strength, and hope.

There are people whose identity has been shielded in this story to protect their anonymity and privacy. You know who you are. Sincere thanks always for all you have done to help my family and bring about the writing of this book.

Grateful thanks to my parents, Marilyn and Jim McCann, for your lifelong example of strength, self-sacrifice, devotion to family, and the power of humor. I feel your presence every day.

A world of thanks to my four beautiful children and son-in-law—sharing life with you is the most precious gift of all.

And to my husband, Joe—my life began the night I met you. You are my world. You are the most humble and courageous person I know. With this book (as with everything in our lives), you always kept me on track, you put things in perspective, you patiently helped with everything large and small, you made me laugh, and you believed in me even when I didn't believe in myself. I love you.

INTRODUCTION

We've heard it said to make your mess your message. That can pose quite a challenge. In the cleaned-up, perfec*tish* world we all aspire to inhabit, who wants the messy parts of their lives hanging like undergarments on a line, flapping in the breeze for the neighbors to see?

There are paradoxes in life. When it comes to the disease of addiction, many hold incredibly true. You must lose your life to save it. You must surrender to win. You must let go to get your loved one back.

This is story about our family, our struggle, and the hope that grew out of that struggle. This is the story of how we learned to live the paradoxes. It is not a pretty one, but it is real and it is ours.

There is an ancient Japanese artistic tradition, known as Kintsugi, that creates beauty from brokenness. In the Kintsugi tradition, broken pottery is repaired with powdered gold mixed into lacquer thus creating golden seams. The underlying philosophy is that an object's cracks and flaws should not be disguised but honored as a part of its history, and thus a more powerful beauty is born through the mend with golden joinery.

The Kintsugi philosophy speaks deeply to the power of recovery. Our family's story is akin to that of a Kintsugi bowl. Addiction broke our family into many pieces, but through God's grace and the many sources of help we have received over the years, we have together found the golden joinery of strength and love.

Our hope is that in sharing our story, other families will find hope, answers, and encouragement, and know that with help they can overcome the devastation of addiction.

Our mess is our message.

A
DECISION

Chapter 1

HANDCUFFED

NANCY

Our son stood with the side of his face pressed up against the outside wall of our home, legs spread wide apart, hands held behind his back with handcuffs. His right hand was broken and swollen from when, in a rage, he punched a hole in a plaster wall of our home the night before. A police officer stood guard at his side to ensure there would be no similar outbursts. JP was too high on drugs to notice. Another police officer walked toward my husband and me, motioning for us to follow him. The three of us stood together about fifty feet away from JP.

The distance between us and our son was greater than a lifetime.

"Look," the police officer said quietly. "We were here at your house last night, and we will keep coming every time you need us. We have enough on him to arrest him. But at some point, you have got to do something. What do you want to do?"

We stood there silently. All I felt was the cold bite of the wind. I was numb with shock, grief, and fear on that brilliant, sunny February noonday. I leaned up against my husband, Joe, and grabbed his arm.

What do you want to do?

The question reverberated in the fear-driven brain freeze of my mind. The night before, the police had escorted JP from our home after a rage-filled confrontation in our kitchen. We told him we would not press charges against him if he agreed to go to rehab for treatment or leave the house for good. It was now the next morning, and he was back. We knew the cycle of substance-induced rage that we all had endured for weeks would begin again if he remained in our home.

Joe and I were on the precipice: severing all ties to JP in the hopes that his solitary free fall would force him to agree to seek help for his substance abuse. Standing next to Joe, I felt like a body encased in stone, trying to move my mouth to say yes to the decision that had borne down on us for months like a massive train roaring down the tracks in the night.

What do you want to do?

There was no turning back. Police cars lined our driveway, spilling out on the street near our home, and JP stood in that interminable distance a few feet away, handcuffed and high.

The police officer's voice broke the silence.

"I know they explained to you about the order of protection, and I know this is hard to do to your own son. We have enough to arrest him now. It's up to you."

He leaned in closer and spoke softly.

"I have a son. He got into some trouble. I told him that he had to straighten out or leave the house. He continued with what he was doing, and I had to have him leave my home. I had no choice. He could not continue to do what he was doing and live with us."

"Where is your son now?"

"I don't know."

I had seen this man many times on duty. He is a formidable figure—tall, muscular, with a shaved head and a no-nonsense look in his eye. His willingness to lay aside his tough-guy public persona and speak to us on such a deeply personal level was like a tiny feather of hope floating down and resting between the three of us.

His words and the risk he took to share them gave me a push toward clarity and the courage to take the action no parent ever wants to have to take. Joe's eyes met mine. After years and years of trying to help our son, we had arrived at *this moment* and we had to find the strength to follow through.

"You can arrest our son," Joe said quietly. "We will press charges against him."

I turned away as they led JP into the patrol car. I tried to tell a police officer JP's broken hand needed medical attention. My husband touched my arm to quiet me.

"We'll take care of it, ma'am. Just come down to headquarters later to fill out the papers."

Our home was empty then. Thankfully, our three daughters were not in the house for that last ugly scene. Annie was away at college, Molly was at high school, and Grace was in first grade at the elementary school a few blocks away.

The phone rang. I could see from the caller ID it was a friend. She had just heard from another woman, who was not my friend and whose children were in school with Grace, that police cars were parked outside my home *again*.

"Are you all right?"

"Yeah, thanks," I responded flatly. "It's a mess. I've got to go."

I knew the uproar at our house for the last twenty-four hours would probably be a lead story for this day's news cycle at book clubs and school pickups in the neighborhood. *That* realization added more brick and mortar to the already heavy walls of isolation I had felt for a long, long time.

But there was no time to ruminate on the fact that there were so very few people I could trust. I threw my exhausted body into a chair and tried to make some sense out of *what the hell had happened.*

Years and years of terrible circumstances had been building and building to a dangerous tipping point. The night before JP's arrest, our home was a tinderbox ready to burst into flame. Anything could have set off what happened. But this time, the match igniting the blaze was the issue of money that JP believed was owed him.

After JP failed out of high school, a family friend kindly tried to help him get back on track by offering him a low-level job at his company. JP showed up for that job for maybe a week. However, in JP's strung-out head, he was owed a lot of money. So, hopped up on some dangerous combination of pills, JP went to the friend's home to demand money.

There wasn't a worse idea to be found in the world that night.

JP arrived and pounded on the front door, demanding a paycheck in a loud voice. At some point, he landed back in our kitchen.

Kaboom.

JP's rage escalated, and I began to grow very scared. Joe decided it was time to call the police for help.

We knew we needed to get our two younger daughters out of the house. Molly was crying, and there was fear in Grace's eyes, a deep fear for what she had seen and heard. She wasn't crying. She didn't say a word. She adored her brother. But he was gone. The fear in Grace's dark brown eyes cut to the heart of the truth: JP had to leave the house once and for all. There was nothing more we could do for him until he agreed to seek treatment for his addiction.

Patrol cars with red lights spinning around were parked on the street and in our driveway. A few police officers were standing there, talking on radios. It looked like a crime scene from a movie. But it wasn't a movie; it was our family's reality.

Inside were about ten guys in uniform—a group in the living room with JP and a group with Joe and me in the kitchen, trying to help us to figure out the next move. Things had clearly spiraled out of control, but in some kind of pathetic last-ditch effort for advice, I felt the need to call a counselor JP had seen a few times. I told him the police were at our house.

"Oh, this is bad," he said in a tone that sounded like he was sharing a *great insight* that had somehow eluded me. "You are going to have to throw him out. But look, I am boarding a plane to Florida right now. I've got to go. Good luck."

Good luck.

In the dark procession of difficult moments that I had felt over those years, that "Good luck" was near the top of the list. Joe and I were alone. We were all we had to do this. I tossed up a silent prayer to what felt like a very remote God to please help us all get through this night.

JP

I can't recall what I was upset about. I was so high there are details that are a blur.

I remember walking into the house, already agitated— probably due to the fact I was using a toxic amount of sedatives and stimulants. I used to find it humorous that I was on a toxic combination and would joke about the fact that I might die.

I remember fighting with my mother in the kitchen that night and her getting me aggravated. I remember picking up the hard plastic and metal house phone and smashing it against my face repeatedly, saying: "Look what you're doing to me. Look what you're doing to me."

In my mind, that was the way I could show my mother how upset I was, that it was her fault, and it made *sense*.

Back then, I would fly off the handle at the drop of a pin.

The next thing I remember from that night was a family friend coming into my house and threatening me. He told me that if I ever made Molly, my sister, upset again he would knock my teeth out. I then encouraged him to do it.

When I called his bluff, he stepped away and I got in his face and began screaming at him. I punched the wall next to his head to try to scare him, hitting the beam and shattering my hand.

Looking back now, me being one hundred pounds soaking wet at that time, he could have beaten the shit out of me. But in the morbid, delusional, and rage-filled trance that consumed my life and brain, I didn't care.

As a matter of fact, there was nothing that I really cared about other than drugs. The last thing I did was go over to the glass-paned back door and punch out one of the windows. My fist went through the glass, cutting my already broken and swollen hand.

I can still remember the look the family friend gave me as he walked out like it was yesterday: it was a stare as if he had just seen a child die.

The police then arrived at the house, and I quickly toned

down my antics to avoid jail. I negotiated and reached the agreement with them that I would leave the house and not return.

NANCY

Physically, only the space of the dining room separated us from our son. Metaphysically, light years would have correctly calculated the distance. Strewn over the course of that time was the wreckage of weeks mounting into months, piling up into years of bad choices, broken promises, drugs, anger, confusion, and, underlying all, fear.

As the police questioned us, I sat at the island in our kitchen. It was the center of our home, the place for meals and gatherings. I glanced at the windowsill over the sink. There stood a very old china statue of the Blessed Mother that JP had bought for me at a tag sale when he was in kindergarten. That Blessed Mother had stood watch in the kitchen over our family life for many years: through births, deaths, Friday pizza dinners, celebrations, and homework sessions. Now she was present for one of the most difficult nights of our lives.

For a moment, that beloved statue reminded me that Mary's loving presence was with us even in the chaos that was ripping our family apart. I knew that—for an instant. And then the sense of assurance was gone.

On the refrigerator were a dozen photographs of our family together and Grace's brightly colored paintings from school. But those homely icons of faith, hope, and love didn't mean a damn thing that night. I didn't even know who we were anymore.

It felt like our family was a sham.

Blue uniforms, guns in holsters, scratchy voices coming through radios, and a son riddled with pills, booze, and rage had pushed out any belief I had in the life we had tried to create for our family. The sanctuary of our home was blown to bits: our son was lost, and our lives lost with his.

Joe told the police that we wanted JP to leave and not contact us until he was ready to commit to treatment. The officer in charge very patiently explained to us the process of getting an order of protection from the village court prohibiting JP from returning to our home. We were somewhat familiar with this strategy. Professionals we had been seeing had been advocating for us to take this step.

Up until that night, Joe and I saw the protection order as a measure of last resort we would use when all options had failed to convince JP to seek treatment. Now, in fact, it was a very real choice to protect us from his rage. Joe and I went into the living room to present JP with his choices.

He was slumped in a chair. He was gaunt. The life in his eyes, gone. His skin was pale as flour. For a second, I remembered back to when our only son was a blonde-haired, blue-eyed boy whose energetic antics and sense of humor kept us all laughing. JP was my little man. He was full of energy, fun, curiosity, and more than a bit of unpredictable mischief. And out of the tumble of those qualities that kept us all on our toes came a nickname that stuck—Manzo. Somehow for me it captured the spirit of what I loved about my son's being.

Seeing him there surrounded by police in our own living room, I wanted to grab his arms and plead, "Please stop all of this. Manzo, we love you. Come back to who you were. We'll get you help. Just agree to it." I steeled myself against those memories and those emotions. I could not afford to start crying in the middle of that room.

There was no Manzo that night. He had been gone a long time. What was left was the shell of our son, whose soul had gone into hiding.

Joe calmly told JP he had to leave the house permanently and if he came back, we would press charges against him for harassment and get an order of protection barring him from the property. But, if he would agree, we would bring him that night to rehab for treatment. JP refused the offer and strode out of the house into the night.

The police officers gathered to leave. One young officer was the last to leave.

"You remind me of my mother," he said.

I stood at the door and started to cry.

JP

I left my parents' house and was picked up by one of my buddies. I then continued to go out and use dangerous drugs. I do remember saying to my friend at the beginning of the night: no matter what, don't let me go back to my house. I knew that soon thereafter any semblance of conscience that I had lingering in my sick brain would be lost, and I did not want to be in my home when that happened. But, at the end of the night, I told this friend it was OK to drop me off at my parents' house.

He objected.

I then threatened him, and he complied.

Chapter 2

BIRTHING A SOLUTION

NANCY

After JP left the house, we spoke to our daughters. We tried to assure them everything would be OK for all of us. I prayed silently that what sounded like hollow words would somehow come true.

"Where are you in this mess, God? I sound like a fake telling the girls it's going to be OK. Where are you? What can you do to help?"

That prayer felt like it hit a thick, impenetrable wall set in place by *Uninvolvement from On High* that slammed right back at me with no answer, no solution, no nothing.

We locked all the doors and windows so JP could not find a way to get back in. I asked Joe to set the alarm for 5 a.m., hardly necessary because neither of us slept that night. A few days earlier, I had promised a friend expecting her fourth baby that I would drive her to the hospital before dawn for her scheduled labor inducement. Her husband had an important early morning meeting to attend while she was being admitted and he would then meet up with her at the hospital to be her labor coach.

Throughout that night, as JP was *God knows where doing God knows what*, Joe and I lay silently next to each other in bed in the dark, hammered by images of what had taken place. The comfort there was in knowing I could always count on Joe to be my partner in whatever happened next.

In a situation like ours, you learn to compartmentalize things. A close friend told me I was good at it. When she said that, it struck me as oddly funny—complimenting me for the ability to compartmentalize the completely awful parts of life from the good ones, as if it were a skill like being a good cook. Compartmentalizing was not a skill set I had been seeking to master. Maybe compartmentalizing was part of the denial of how bad things really were at home. Or maybe it was a survival strategy: no matter what, I just need to keep putting one foot in front of the other.

Maybe it was a little of both.

So just before dawn on the morning after *That Awful Night*, I gulped down a strong cup of coffee and drove my very pregnant friend to the hospital. In sticking with the script of compartmentalization, I was determined not to let what happened the night before interfere with the new day dawning and the joy it would bring: the birth of a new baby. And I learned a lasting lesson on *How God Answers Prayer*.

On the morning after *That Awful Night* featuring our raging son and a squad of police swarming our home, I believed that on a macro level not even one of my prayers to God— such as *please turn JP's life around* or *please don't make us have to throw him out on the street in the middle of winter*—had been answered in a long time. In fact, both JP and God seemed alike to me regarding any macro-level pleading I had done. Both seemed to be ignoring my pleas—JP to *get* some help, and, in the case of God Almighty, to *give* some help. But on a micro level, there seemed to be some prayer-answering taking place by a caring God—a very useful thing to know. Armageddon may have invaded my home on *That Awful Night* before, but on *this* day new life was being birthed.

The very act of driving my friend helped push back against the wreckage of the night before. When we got to the birthing room, the doctor, who had delivered my friend's other children, made some jokes about me serving as a midwife, and it helped me for a moment to feel I was more than the complete breakdown of a mother I truly believed I was.

The birthing room became flooded with bright morning sunlight. My friend's husband arrived soon after, and the three of us sat together waiting. There was God's glory in the waiting, too. And it was strong enough and apparent enough for me to feel it in my sleep-deprived and grieving state. More prayer answering—and maybe not so micro after all.

Around 11 a.m., my cell phone rang. It was Joe. I knew the good feelings of the birthing room were about to come to a dead halt.

"Nancy, he's back," Joe said. "He's sleeping in the barn. I think he climbed in through the window. We are going to have to take this to the next level."

I didn't show my friends the fear I felt. I told them Joe called to wish them well. I hugged my friend tightly and headed for home. Driving back, I tried to steel myself for the inevitable.

But really, there is nothing in the Parenting Handbook we are all supposed to receive at the birth of a child to prepare you for the moment you consent to having that child arrested.

JP

When I got home after my friend dropped me off, I tried to enter the house—but over the months, my parents had screwed down every window, and every door had multiple locks. My previous attempts and successes at breaking into their home were not going to work this time. I then turned my clouded attention to the barn next to my parents' house and used one of my mother's gardening tools to pry open the window. I climbed into the bed and went to sleep.

I was awakened the next morning by my mother and father informing me that the police were on their way. I remember thinking I really didn't care and all I wanted to do was sleep. The next time I woke up was probably about twenty minutes later—and it was to the sound of a police radio. I was handcuffed shortly after.

NANCY

Joe was waiting for me in the driveway. I told him I wanted to try to tell JP one last time that he needed to seek help for his addiction. There were two things going on inside of me: fear that we had actually come to the moment of reckoning with JP, and the *Secret Belief*. Throughout all the years of JP's free fall, I shared this secret with no one—not even Joe—because as things got worse, this *Secret Belief* just seemed crazier and crazier. And it was this: *somehow, somewhere, God was going to step in with big feet and a freaking miracle was going to happen in JP's life.*

Let me be crystal clear: this *Secret Belief* about God's action was different from denial. It was something *embedded* in my soul. All along the torturous road we had travelled together, I kept thinking JP was going to be *Struck from On High*—like Saul encountering God while riding his horse on the road to Damascus or like Bill W., co-founder of AA, experiencing the power of a transforming light releasing him from his alcoholism. The *Secret Belief* was that an instantaneous miracle was going to happen, and JP was going to be changed.

Deep inside, I kept believing that *something was going to spiritually wake that boy up and he would come back to us restored, sober, and smiling*. I felt this belief in my bones. I kept looking for *that moment* when it would happen—a spiritual awakening hitting JP like a bolt of lightning.

What I didn't realize the morning we had JP arrested was that the *Secret Belief* would eventually happen. But not for many years. What I didn't realize that morning was that the torment of the tough-love stance of throwing him out of our house into the cold would be the beginning of the *Answer to Prayers*. The chaos of those days when we finally cut him off was a gift—a very dark gift—but a gift nevertheless because it opened the path for a new way of life for us all together.

Our oldest daughter, Annie, was intuitive enough to sense that I was holding out for some divine intervention, and, because she was really angry about the whole situation and had pretty much given up hope for her brother, she felt duty bound to set the record straight. To really cut to the heart of the matter and help me to see how far things had fallen off the face of the earth, she used JP's nickname to make her point.

"You think you are going to get your Manzo back? Well it's never going to happen. So just forget about it. Your Manzo is gone. He's not coming back. And the sooner you realize that, the better off we will all be."

Annie definitely had a point—just not one I wanted to hear.

Still I persevered. I felt all God had to do was snap his *Almighty* fingers and JP would be restored. It seemed so simple and logical to me—in a crazed, deep-in-my-soul sort of way.

But it was apparent on the morning of February 18, 2008, that there would be no such dazzling solution. We had reached the end of the line of every effort: special schools, tutors, therapists, psychiatrists, antidepressants, wilderness programs, mentors, moderators, priests, counselors, coaches, behavior contracts, threats, punishments, social workers, rewards, wizards, coaxing, yelling, and silence.

As an addict, JP was a threat to himself and to others, and we needed to take a drastic step that would hopefully save him from self-destruction. It was clear, and it was time.

Yet, the rescuer in me still wanted to try to reason with him one more time.

Go ahead. Call me Cleopatra, the Queen of Denial.

I deserved it.

I went into the room where he was asleep on the bed. His skinny frame was curled up in a fetal position, with his clothes and black ski jacket still on. The room was very cold. His skin was so pale he looked translucent. My throat tightened with emotion because he looked like a corpse on that bed, dressed in black.

I shook his shoulder.

"Wake up, JP. You can't stay here. You need to leave. Wake up."

JP opened his eyes, which were still as blue as the ocean on a summer day. He muttered that I needed to leave him alone.

"JP, you need to leave. We will call the police, and you will be arrested if you don't get out of here."

More muttering.

Then panic started to set in. I knew what was coming, and I was desperate to avoid it for all of us.

"Pleeeeeasssse, JP. Please leave. We are going to call the police."

"Just let me sleep."

I walked outside, and Joe called the police. I felt I was being sawed in two with the jagged edge of a rusty knife. Half of me wanted to find the courage to follow through with the plan: arrest JP for trespassing to force him to seek help for his addiction. The other half—the half of me that still couldn't fathom how bad it all was—wanted to find what the AA Big Book calls an "easier, softer way" in the hopes of sparing all of us the pain of this last resort.

I didn't see then that the pain we were all living in was *far worse* than the action of the actual arrest. It just went against every one of my natural, maternal instincts to do this to my own son. The police were just minutes away.

In my panicked, crazed-mother state of mind, I caved in to trying to save him one last time. I *hate* to admit this, but I went back into the room again to try to get him out in those last moments before the police arrived. It was desperate of me, pathetically desperate.

I shook his sleeping body hard.

"The police have been called, JP. Get out of here. Please go. Run. Leave."

Nothing. It was like trying to wake the dead.

I walked outside again. Freezing air slapped my face and snapped some reality into my brain. Within seconds the police cars were lining the road and the driveway, just as they had the night before. I looked at Joe. He was ready for this, and I knew I had to pull myself together and be ready too.

What we didn't know then was that day would be the last time the police ever came to our home because of a problem with JP. Our family had in fact lurched into a solution, not the way we would have chosen, but the way that was *necessary* for us. And ultimately, it provided the groundwork for building the solution piece by piece.

"For I know the plans I have for you," declares the Lord, "plans to prosper you and not to harm you, plans to give you hope and a future" (Jer 29:11).

If someone had told me that Old Testament verse that day, I would have been mightily annoyed. I hate when people cheerfully rattle off Scripture or say, "Everything is going to work out," in the midst of a broken situation they aren't in. While their efforts are well intentioned, they come off as clueless to me. Sometimes it's better to hold a holy, empathic *silence*—as in keep your cheerful Scripture rattling to yourself because I don't want to hear it right now. But with the benefit of years, I have come to realize that verse was truly applicable to all of us; I just didn't have the eyes to see it or the heart to feel it then.

Maybe someone else gifted with great faith and great trust could have had the vision to grasp that promise God made to Jeremiah and apply it to his or her life in a similar circumstance. But I am definitely not gifted with great faith and great trust. All I ever had was the gift of perseverance and attention to moments when God's "still, small voice" guided us, most of the time through the flesh-and-blood love of others.

God had a plan to give us all "hope and a future." It was unfolding. Harsh as it sounds, the unfolding started the day we had JP arrested.

I just didn't know it at the time.

Later at the police station, we gave our statements and the charges against our son were formally written up. Any shred of the bandage of denial was ripped off. The police officers listened as we explained what happened at our home in those last forty-eight hours. Somewhere in the haze of fear, exhaustion, and denial, I heard my voice stating it, as if I was having an out-of-body experience. I heard my voice confirm that JP had committed crimes against us. Giving the police our statements effectively destroyed what was left of any misguided protectiveness we had for our son. I saw, through the eyes of the law enforcement officer writing down our accounts, just how *far down* this had taken all of six of us.

I was crushed by the fact that absolutely nothing we had done helped our son change the course of his life. I believed I had miserably failed at the most important work of my life: being a mother. That sense of failure stayed with me for a long time—years, in fact.

But there was a moment of grace, too. I felt a tiny flicker of hope that maybe, just maybe, this action of last resort was the right path to take. It was a tiny flicker assuring me that we had followed the best guidance we could get, with the right intention in our hearts. There was comfort in that hope, and I was grateful I didn't miss it during all the turmoil and now exhaustion.

JP was scheduled to be at the court at 7 p.m. Sometime before dinner, we learned that my friend gave birth to a beautiful baby boy.

Great news. Then it was back to reality.

I threw together a bag of clothes to give JP. The reason was twofold: we did not want him to have any excuse for coming back; and with a forecast looming for a significant snowstorm, I wanted to make sure he had warm clothes for wherever he landed. In the grand plan, the clothes bag was a useless effort. Joe and I also knew we could not be involved with helping JP in any way with legal representation. We were clueless as to how it would play out at the arraignment. Panic (again) started to set in just as we were about to enter the courtroom.

What would happen to him? Would bail be set? Would he have to go to jail? Who was going to represent him? Where would he go? Was he going to come out of this alive?

Chapter 3

HOMELESS

NANCY

As I reached out to open the courtroom door—with all those fearful questions living rent-free in my head—my cell phone rang. It was Kathy, one of my most beloved friends and a woman of deep faith, who works as an attorney. She knew what had been going on for months. I trusted her completely and was ready to do whatever she suggested.

"Kath, thank God you called," I choked out. "We had JP arrested today. We are standing outside the court to go in for his arraignment. What if bail is set and he can't make bail? What happens?"

Kathy's voice was calm and firm.

"There are worse things in life than spending a night in the county jail," she stated. "Do what you have to do, Nancy. I am praying for all of you. It will be OK."

There were only five people in the courtroom. The judge assigned to cover the holiday weekend was Justice Patrick, a member of our parish. I had served on the Parish Council with him, and we taught together in our church program for high school students. While I felt embarrassed for Judge Patrick to see our family in shambles, I knew him to be fair and kind. His presence on the bench made the arraignment seem slightly less surreal.

Some people have this amazing connection with angels. I am not big on invoking the presence of angels. They don't really swoop around me in daily life the way they do for others. But Judge Patrick as the presider in the court that night and in the months following as the case went forward had a *guardian angel quality* to it. It was a reminder God was some-where in the mess, watching out for all of us.

Judge Patrick glanced over at Joe and me, and for a moment I saw the wisdom and compassion in his eyes that I had seen many other times in our church work together. He released JP without bail on the condition he appear in court during the regular calendar two days later. JP agreed, and just that fast it was over. We tried to hand him the bag of clothes as he walked out of the courtroom, but he brushed past us as if we were invisible.

JP

After getting booked into the local precinct, I was still so high from the night before I continued to sleep until my court appearance that evening.

I stood in front of the judge, and I can't tell you anything he said or told me to do. The only words I remember hearing were I would be out and free that night.

I didn't care about jail. I didn't care about my family, friends, or relatives— I didn't care about anyone or anything except for drugs. The judge gave me a court order, a yellow sheet of paper ordering me to check in for state-mandated drug and IOP (Intensive Out Patient treatment). If I failed to do so, I would have violated the terms of my release and be sent immediately to jail.

That night I lit the piece of paper on fire.

I was delusional. I aspired to be the worst person I could be. I felt that laws and society's rules had no bearing on life, nor did I have to follow them. Looking back, if I had dealt with someone who was the same low-life person I was, I would have ordered him to be in jail for a long, long time.

The only thing that held any interest for me in any way at all was drugs. Everything aside from drugs, ways to get drugs, or new drugs to try would not remain in my mind for more than a second. During the time I was in active addiction, there were many life-threatening and dangerous scenarios that transpired.

The reason I am explaining this is because I am thinking of how I almost went to jail that night, but it didn't matter. *That's how powerful this thing is.*

NANCY

We now entered new, uncharted territory, completely cutting ties with our son as a form of leverage to get him to seek help for his addiction to alcohol and pills. Someone told us: "You are starving him out."

All of us were depleted. Twelve-step programs tell you addiction is a physical, mental, and spiritual disease. As it is a disease that sickens an entire family, all six of us were, in some way, subject to those three levels of illness. Joe and I became a kind of disaster-relief team, trying to clean up what the AA Big Book calls "wreckage" strewn across all our lives.

When Molly went back to school the next day, she found her life further upended by the grapevine of other students asking her what had happened to her brother. Molly was incredibly upset by this freewheeling gossip and called me from school to say that stories were buzzing around and what should she do? This is where the truth about the statement *hostage-taking* becomes apparent. Molly was working very hard at living parallel existences: an incredibly volatile life at home and her "normal" life as a high school sophomore. She was adept at the skill of compartmentalizing, too.

But now any semblance of security Molly had created for herself at school was compromised—and the two worlds she had worked so hard to keep apart collided together. I was desperate to protect Molly. I called a teacher, and he promised to keep Molly close.

Then I got in the car and drove to the police station. I was on a mission. There was something else I needed to do to tamp down the buzz. I asked to speak to the police chief, and he kindly saw me right away. I thanked him for the professionalism that the department's officers had used in helping us. He began by trying to reassure me that what was happening in our home was not uncommon and that we had done the right thing. I appreciated his words.

As a former newspaper journalist, I knew incidents reported in the police blotter were always fodder for gossip once published in the newspapers. I also knew there is always some discretionary power a department has in releasing information to the press. I asked him to limit the release of information to the local paper about our son's arrest. He promised to make every effort to maintain our family's privacy. He was a man of his word.

While we were trying to contain the damage on one end of our lives, we were going after a hard-hitting solution to the problem on other fronts. So, while JP was initially living in a flophouse, then downgrading even further to sleeping in a car, we went to the first of our meetings with the county Domestic Violence Unit (DVU). This was a daunting task, made easier because we were accompanied by Joe's oldest friend, Jimmy, who is an attorney.

A few years before, Jimmy had gone through a difficult time requiring him to take some tough-love measures to help one of his own children. Jimmy candidly shared with us his experience and how it resulted in a positive and lasting change for his adult child. He felt a great deal of empathy for our family. He understood from the inside what we were going through. He spoke to us without judgment or criticism. He gave us his full support and honest assessment of what we needed to do.

Jimmy's presence was invaluable and a clear demonstration of *How God Answers Frantic Prayers*. We needed help and he showed up for us. Joe had known Jimmy from the time their mothers, who were best friends, strolled them side-by-side in baby carriages. Jimmy had been in our wedding party. We had both been in his. Our families had shared many milestones together—births, deaths, weddings, and parties celebrating the sacraments of our children. Sitting with him in the waiting area outside Family Court, I was grateful for his willingness to be with us and help us.

Kathy, Jimmy, and Judge Patrick did not have angel wings growing out of their backs or halos levitating over their heads. But they were guiding forces for us, flesh-and-blood embodiments of *How God Shows Up*. Scripture has a lot of stories about mystical beings appearing out of the blue to offer guidance to completely clueless human beings whom God, for some reason I can't even fathom, chose to use to roll out his salvation plan. Joseph's life plan probably didn't initially include marrying a pregnant virgin, receiving shepherds and mysterious Magi to celebrate Jesus' birth, and then fleeing to Egypt to protect his newborn foster son from a power-crazed murderer intent on killing all boys two years and under in the vicinity of Bethlehem. An "angel of the Lord" appeared to Joseph in dreams to guide him to take Mary as his wife, commanded him to flee town as Herod's infanticide bore down, and finally announced the coast was clear for the Holy Family.

That's a whole lot of angelic appearances.

I always kind of secretly wished I could see an angel the way Joseph did. It would have been great to get a heavenly *Two-For-One Deal*: a good night's sleep and some incredibly divine guidance from an angel, *maybe* with some radiant light shooting out of his hands, in a Joseph-like prophetic dream to point out the direction our family needed to go when everything was falling apart.

That wish never came true.

But, lo and behold, these many years later, I realize there were angels around all the while. They just wore street clothes, appeared in real time during waking hours, and had names like Kathy, Judge Patrick, and Jimmy.

Where would we have been without them?

At our meeting with the DVU, there was no getting around the cold, hard facts of the threatening behavior JP had engaged in against us. Our conversations with the DVU bureau chief helped us to understand even more clearly the issue of domestic violence that was front and center in our home when our son was high.

The levels of denial we construct to avoid the truth of addiction and how it destroys both the addict and the family are powerful. Denial is the stranglehold preventing both the addict and the family from doing what is most necessary: admitting the dangerous unmanageability of addictive behavior and getting help for it.

JP was addicted to an escalating variety of substances. In a real sense, I was addicted to the situation of trying to save him from the consequences of his own poor choices.

And that's what is called the dance of codependence.

I did not see it then, but looking back, the gift of those first days after JP's arrest was that we were forced to confront the truth of how deeply we were immersed in the roiling depths of this disease. And like JP, we had to *make a choice* to change our behavior to save our family.

The host body of the disease of addiction is the family system. If addiction is a tumor, then an enabling family serves as the veins and capillaries that feed the tumor, allowing it to grow. We as a family had to cut off whatever was sustaining JP's addict life. The first step was extricating ourselves from the deceptive web of enabling our son. Those bitter February days were the beginning of working toward a new solution.

We were advised by counseling professionals to get everything lined up so that when JP did decide to literally come in from the cold and seek help in rehab, we would be ready. We contacted our insurance provider to get preapproval for a treatment center and began to research places for JP to go. Joe and I made a lot of phone calls to people whose judgment we trusted to collect information about good places for treatment.

We zeroed in on a place in South Florida. It had a good reputation, it was far enough away that it would be difficult for JP to leave once there, and it took our insurance plan. We even knew the schedule of flights to South Florida from the local airport that JP could use to get down there. Those activities kept us somewhat occupied during the day.

We waited for him to call, and we prayed the Rosary together each night. That was about all we could do on those long nights when we did not know where our son was, or even if he was alive.

Chapter 4

COMBAT

JP

There was now a restraining order preventing me from being within 100 yards of my family. This gave me all the more reason to be a menace. I was quickly able to find a place to stay that evening at a friend's house. He was kind enough to let me sleep on his couch. That night, I don't know if it really was a suicide attempt, but I took enough drugs to kill myself.

I didn't care if I died.

I ingested four Xanax bars, one gram of cocaine, three oxycodone, six beers—and before I went to sleep, I smoked a couple of blunts and sniffed two Ambien.

I remember laying my head down on this plastic fake-leather couch and not caring if I ever woke up from the deep sleep I was about to take.

When I watch movies about murderers, criminals, or other dark-themed genres, I can identify so much with the characters and scenery because I unfortunately lived some of that horror for years of my life.

The person I was afraid of becoming is the person I am happy to call myself today. This is not an embellishment or glorification of the way I used to be. It's the harsh reality of the downward spiral and subsequent resurrection of my life.

NANCY

During the day I could push from my mind the terror I felt by trying to busy myself with daily routines. But at night, the activity slowed down and fear took over.

Where is he? What is he doing? Who is he with? Is he going to die?

Joe and I would be sleepless in the middle of the night. We spoke in shorthand in the dark.

"Joe?"

"Nancy . . . we just may get a phone call. . . . If we do, we did everything we could."

"I know."

Joe often prayed the Rosary silently before going to sleep. My husband is the core of balance and strength in all our lives. His soft-spoken voice attracted me the minute I met him. Joe truly had me at hello. His inner strength has always protected all of us. Throughout this chaotic challenge, he was calm and resolute. I was the frayed nerve ending.

I wish I could say I was some kind of phenomenal prayer warrior amid the uncertainty.

But that would be a big lie.

The fact is that week, the many months before *that* week, and for a couple of years after *that* week, I found it very difficult to pray. Some classic spiritual literature describes this as a time of testing in a spiritual desert. The desert image never did much for me. A desert is quiet, and you can be left alone—which seems a hell of a lot better than being surrounded by yelling and threats.

The image that stuck with me was always a densely overgrown spiritual jungle, which I could not hack my way out of, filled with strangling vines, quicksand, poisonous snakes, and ferocious man- and/or woman-eating wild beasts.

Yes, that was more like it.

And in that jungle location, I had a very hard time praying.

I possessed all the credentials to spiritually meet these challenges. I had taken all kinds of classes on meditation, prayer, Scripture, and spirituality in graduate school at Fordham University to earn a degree in spiritual direction. I read piles of books on faith and spirituality and was a teacher in our parish religious education program. I was a card-carrying member of a 12-step program for eighteen sober years. I knew slogans like "Let Go and Let God."

But none of it did much good. All the good stuff just wasn't that accessible to me in helping to feel at peace with the circumstances.

I couldn't consistently find the part of my being that could believe and trust God would make good on his promise to get our family through this. I kept wanting to see the *Footprints* story about being carried by God through the difficult times become a reality in my own life. But it wasn't happening. The fact is there were a lot of moments when it felt like God had completely dropped us.

With the benefit of time, I now realize God did carry and protect all of us. But in the midst of all the unraveling taking place, anxiety, fear, regret, guilt, and anger went after me like a five-headed Hydra. It was a time of desolation, as described by St. Ignatius Loyola, founder of the Jesuits, in "The Spiritual Exercises," written 500 years ago.

I was lost in that desolation, but I knew enough from my studying the "Exercises" at Fordham—and from my longtime spiritual director, Sister Kathleen—that St. Ignatius recommends a person battle against desolation.

"[T]he enemy characteristically weakens, loses courage, and flees with his temptations when the person engaged in spiritual endeavors stands bold and unyielding against the enemy's temptations and goes diametrically against them."[1]

The image of being "bold and unyielding" in prayer really appealed to me. It even empowered me for brief stretches of time. While outside circumstances rendered me weak, I could still aspire to be some kind of kick-ass prayer warrior princess—like a spiritual Wonder Woman—battling desolation. St. Paul's exhortations to the young Church in Ephesus gave great imagery to outfit the prayer warrior princess part of me.

"Finally, be strong in the Lord and in his mighty power. Put on the full armor of God, so that you can take your stand against the devil's schemes. . . . Stand firm then, with the belt of truth buckled around your waist, with the

---

[1]   Ignatius of Loyola, *Ignatius of Loyola: The Spiritual Exercises and Selected Works*, ed. George E. Ganss, S.J. (Mahwah, NY: Paulist Press, 1991), 204.

breastplate of righteousness in place, and with your feet fitted with the readiness that comes from the gospel of peace. . . . Take the helmet of salvation and the sword of the Spirit, which is the word of God" (Eph 6:10–11, 14–15, 17).

Oh yeah.

I tapped into memories of when prayer worked and very deliberately followed spiritual practices that brought me comfort and clarity in the past. Again, St. Ignatius was my guide. The flip side of desolation is consolation, which he describes as:

> *"Every increase in hope, faith, and charity, and every interior joy which calls and attracts one toward heavenly things and to the salvation of one's soul, by bringing it tranquility and peace in its Creator and Lord."*[2]

I sought out those practices that increased faith, hope and charity in my life to shove back the desolation. Sometimes the shove back worked. But the fighting spirit of the prayer warrior princess never lasted for very long. I was just grateful for when it did.

One practice that worked was saying the Rosary. The tactile experience of holding rosary beads and repeating the words of the Hail Mary was a great source of comfort. When I was single, I learned the power of praying the Rosary when my godfather, Uncle Harold, asked me to commit with him to praying the Rosary every day to meet a "fine young man." I had recently come off a train-wreck break up. Uncle Harold was a retiree living in Florida, and I was in New York trying to get a career as a journalist off the ground. We stayed connected through handwritten, snail-mail letters and our shared faith and prayer intention.

"There's power in "The Beads," he wrote. "Pray "The Beads."

I did. A month later I met Joe.

---

2   Ignatius of Loyola, 202

Developing a faith connection with the Blessed Mother through the Rosary helped bring Joe and I back to the Catholic Church when we were parents of a young family. The Blessed Mother was a sweet and comforting presence during that wonderful season of our lives. Now I tethered myself to "The Beads" to cobble together some peace.

Another source of consolation was the Sacrament of Penance. Did I really want to bare my soul and share my shortcomings with a priest in a confessional? Initially I thought I would rather get my teeth drilled at the dentist. I entered the confessional at church wracked with regret and apprehension.

But I found speaking honestly to a compassionate priest and receiving absolution lifted my sense of failure. Somehow the sacrament gave me comfort, strength, and hopefulness. I always felt *renewed*, which surprised me at first. I thought maybe it was just a coincidence. But over time, I realized the sacrament lived up to its promise of providing strength for the journey and a greater sense of union with Christ's loving heart.

Eucharistic Adoration was another big gun in the arsenal against hopelessness. Joe and I frequently went to the tiny chapel in our church, open for business 24/7—just like a favorite all-night diner, except the menu offers only two house specialties: the presence of Christ in the Eucharist on the altar, and complete silence. We live directly across the street from our church. So it has always been easy to walk there any time.

I immediately feel a sense of peace entering the chapel. It penetrates me the way warmth does after being out in the cold for too long. The chapel's peace is enveloping, and I *know* I have entered another dimension. It's the power of Christ's Eucharistic presence and all the prayers offered hour after hour, day after day, year after year.

Saint Teresa of Calcutta and her Missionaries of Charity set aside a chunk of time to pray each day before the Eucharist to prepare for their work with the poorest of the poor, the sick, and the dying. If prayer before the Eucharist fueled Saint Teresa, then I wanted some of that fuel, too.

Spiritual practices weren't the only things keeping us going during those days. God kept sending us a steady supply of companions on the journey. Their presence in our lives was a flesh-and-blood answer to our prayers. Christ told his followers at the Last Supper, "This is my body. This is my blood," and gave us himself in the Eucharist.

In much the same way, Christ's presence is with us in the embodiment of those who show up for us when we feel the most alone.

A prayer attributed to St. Teresa of Avila says it well:

"Christ has no body now but yours. No hands, no feet on earth but yours. Yours are the eyes through which he looks compassion on this world. Yours are the feet with which he walks to do good. Yours are the hands through which he blesses all the world. Yours are the hands, yours are the feet, yours are the eyes, you are his body. Christ has no body now on earth but yours."

I wanted an immediate answer from God in the form of a big-time, sparkly miracle, but I knew that wasn't going to happen. We were deep in a process. Over time I learned that the *Answers to Prayer Process* came in the form of dear family members and friends who loved, encouraged, and supported all of us even if it looked a hell of a lot like a huge, hot mess. They lived out St. Teresa's prayer for us. They were Christ's hands, feet, eyes, and loving heart for us as we struggled.

Two phone calls made from distances bookended our days and helped us maintain our resolve.

Joe's older brother, Bob, lived more than 4,000 miles away in Hawaii, but that did not prevent him from sticking close. Bob offered unconditional support and good counsel for his godson, JP, and for us. He called every single night when JP was living on the street, encouraging us to be resolute in our decision not to let him back in. He told us over and over that he believed his godson would eventually turn his life around.

Every morning our dearest family friend, Tina, who lives 100 miles away on the far tip of eastern Long Island, called us. Before moving to Long Island, Tina and her family were our next-door neighbors for fifteen years. I always believed God had a special plan in mind when pairing our families. We moved next to Tina and her family three days before JP was born. I was nine months pregnant, with big boxes filling every room of the house, and Tina showed up at the back door with a big pot of homemade chicken soup. Something happened in that moment. The grace of friendship knit our hearts together right there on the spot, and ever since, she has been someone whom my family deeply treasures.

Every year on JP's birthday, December 22, our families celebrated together with a big Italian dinner and homemade cake made by Tina, who is an incredible cook. She loves our family like her own. She watched as things fell apart and knew something drastic had to be done.

During those days after JP's arrest, Tina kept a close eye despite the miles between us. She spoke to me with loving firmness. She told me not to back down. Sometimes we cried together on the phone. But she always ended every conversation telling me the words her own mother-in-law always told her, "Listen to me. You stay strong in your mind. You stay strong in your mind and body."

On the third day of what I think of now as a standoff, there was a blizzard and it just about put me over the edge. The thought of my child (yes, my *adult* child, my *addicted adult* child, but my *child* nonetheless) homeless in the snow was incomprehensible.

Tina called and pretty much yelled at me in her thick Bronx accent.

"Don't you back down now, Nancy. You see this through. Do you hear me? Don't you stop. You have got to be strong in your mind."

Tina can always pack a punch when she needs to, but her words were not just tough talk. She and her husband, Joe, had buried their youngest daughter, Janine, just few years earlier. Tina stood strong with Janine, caring for her as she courageously battled against leukemia. Our family had the privilege of being part of that journey with Tina's family. I knew Tina was trying to cement strength into me. It was strength I did not believe I had, though I realize now I did, thanks to her.

Joe, whose soft-spoken kindness and gentleness won my heart when we were dating so many years before, overheard my conversation with Tina and reinforced it.

He pointed his finger and said, "Don't go soft on me. Do *not* go soft on me now."

A phone call at that time from my brother, Jim, stands out in my mind.

"Look, Nancy," he said, "you can't think of it as having JP arrested. You have to think of this as using the last tool you have available to force your son to get help. You did this because you love your son, not because you want to punish him. You are leveraging the only thing you have left to use to get him the help he needs. It's leverage, Nance. That's all it is."

His words have stayed with me over the years, and I share them now with parents who are looking for help for their addicted adult children. Those parents need some real-time angels, too.

Chapter 5

RABIES

NANCY

Homeless and hungry in the blizzard, JP called the house and asked if he could shovel our driveway in exchange for some food. Almost robotically, I repeated the words I had been instructed to say.

"By court order you are not allowed to contact us or come to the house. If you want to seek help for your addiction, we will get you on a plane to a detox and rehab. Otherwise do not contact us."

Heart pounding, I hung up the phone.

JP

After the first night in my buddy's house, I woke up to getting told I had to leave—I could not stay there anymore. I thought that the night before I had fallen asleep immediately from all the drugs I had taken. But now I was being told that in my drug-infested stupor, I had robbed this kid's house.

I kind of recalled taking things and leaving to sell them that night, but it was all pretty much a blur.

I remember leaving his house in the morning seeing that a big water jug he used for a coin jar, which had been filled with change when I was at the house the night before, was now empty.

That was the type of person I was. The second I took any mood- or mind-altering chemical, I was liable to do anything—even to people who were giving me a place to crash for the night.

I then enlisted the help of another buddy. He had it more together than I did. He let me sleep in his car. I can't pinpoint what happened which night, but to summarize: those nights, there was heavy drug use and a lot of theft.

I can recall walking into a gas station in the wee hours of the night, saying hello to the attendant and smiling at him while I filled my pockets with whatever I wanted. And when he told me he would call the police, I told him I would fucking kill him. This was a normal occurrence for me. I would confidently go to a gas station I frequented the night before and be asked to leave for some sort of disturbance or theft I had committed the previous day.

It was difficult for me to understand that I was doing these things, that it was my fault and my actions that were reaping the repercussions. My sick and twisted thinking blamed everyone else. It wasn't because I stole from the gas station and cursed at the guy that I wasn't allowed back. My delusional thinking had me believe the guy was an asshole and *that* was why I wasn't allowed in the store.

In that mindset, I was capable of justifying anything. And I honestly believed most of the distortions.

My brain was not centered on the truth.

Being addicted is like having rabies. Raccoons are instinctively nocturnal animals. But when infected with rabies, they don't know if it's day or night and they roam the streets during the daytime against their natural instincts. They are stumbling around in a strange manner, drooling and foaming at the mouth. They are sick, and the sickness is centered in their rabid brains. The rabies-infested raccoon probably thinks it's behaving normally, but to anyone who observes it, it is whacked out.

But it doesn't know it.

To me, in my addicted mind, my life was normal. But, I was like the rabid raccoon who thought he was living normally; almost everyone who saw me knew I was very sick and every behavior and thought process I experienced went against normal human instincts. This sort of thinking applied to all areas of my previous addicted life: every burned-down building, every messed-up relationship and negative consequence was—in my twisted mind—a result of the person who was the victim in the situation and not the offender—me.

This sickness was so powerful that I infected people around me. For example, my mother had to say and do things she never would have, because of my illness. Unfortunately, an animal with rabies must be put down. And although I probably behaved in a fashion that deserved *that* consequence, there was light at the end of the tunnel.

If you had asked me then if I could see the light at the end of the tunnel, I would have told you no. Being on the other side of things now, I would never want to go back to that life.

NANCY

Unbeknownst to us, JP was violating the order of protection by calling Molly on her cell phone. But she never told on her brother. JP asked Molly to get him food. She has always been the true heart of our family. She was stuck between a rock and a hard place: her brother pleading for help and her parents telling her there was a court order demanding JP stay away. Molly went with her heart and snuck food, clothes, and even a coin collection down to the bottom of our driveway, leaving it in the mailbox for JP to pick up.

More than a week went by. I woke up early one morning and was drinking a cup of coffee in our living room, trying to figure out how I would get through the day. I hadn't slept or eaten much for days. My body felt as if it had been put through a meat grinder. The phone rang, and I answered it, thinking Tina was calling me.

I was wrong. On the other end was a woman yelling at me in a loud, angry voice.

"What kind of mother are you? What kind of person are you to let your son sleep in a car? Why don't you come down here and take care of your problems instead of leaving them for me?"

The caller then identified herself as the mother of one of JP's friends. Apparently after several days with no place to stay, JP slept on her son's bedroom floor for a night. She told JP he needed to go home, and he then began sleeping in her son's car in the snow. I tried to explain we had offered JP the opportunity to go to rehab to get help. She yelled over me, saying I didn't need to send my son away, I had no business forcing him to leave our home, and I just needed to listen to my son and provide him with a good home.

Her words hurt me terribly. They zeroed in on my greatest fear: we had failed as parents. I thanked the woman for helping JP, and got off the phone.

Something broke inside me. My body was shaking, and I realized I could not go on with this standoff.

My sense of resolve and commitment were completely upended. I decided to tell Joe I was *done*; we could get JP a room at the YMCA and work from that point. The phone rang again and this time it was Tina. I was crying so hard, I could barely speak. I told her I could not continue with what we were doing.

I know Tina heard something in my voice that worried her.

"Nancy, I understand. I will support you on this," she said softly.

Joe walked into the living room. He was talking on his cell phone. He gestured to me that he was talking to JP.

"Ok," Joe said. "I will call you back with the time of your flight."

I couldn't believe what I was hearing. I told Tina.

"Thank God. Thank God. Go take care of it," she said.

At the *exact moment* I was giving up, JP had given up too and called Joe to help him get to rehab. For the first time in a long time, I felt God's action directly intervening by the timing of JP's decision and his phone call home.

JP

I opened my eyes, wrapped in my down jacket, shivering and trying to piece together where I was, realizing after a few minutes that I was still sleeping in my friend's car in the snow.

At this point, my brain was removed from drugs for a few

hours, which gave me a window for my quiet conscience to chime in. The thought barreled through my brain and then vanished faster than lightning: *Maybe* they are right. *Maybe* I do have a problem. *Maybe* being homeless at nineteen years old, sleeping in a car, is not where my destiny is meant to be. *Maybe* I should stop using drugs. *Maybe* I haven't been such a great person recently.

Looking back, I could hear my conscience and all these *maybes* because I was in a great amount of pain.

The fact is the delusional fortress I had made in my mind that everything was OK, that everyone else was to blame, and that I didn't have a problem had been struck down by an enormous cannonball. The cold, harsh weather I woke up to that morning in the car did not even compare to the cold, harsh reality I woke up to—my conscience.

This seemed to be the end of the road for me.

As I walked up the stairs to my friend's apartment, 1,001 thoughts were racing through my mind. Most of them had to do with different schemes to get my next fix.

I had an immense amount of pain in my core. In my gut, I was crumbling. The only way I could describe this feeling is to compare it to grieving the death of a very dear loved one. Everything I ever loved, everything I ever held dear, anything that ever brought a smile to my face, now was completely shattered.

And I felt as if I was rolling in the shattered glass.

My parents had suggested I go to rehab for quite some time. And in my mind, they were the ones who needed therapy and rehab because they had the problem. They needed help—not me. I believed this even though I was stealing, lying, cheating, and ingesting drugs on an hourly basis. I was afraid of life, afraid of feelings, and afraid of failure. So, I had decided instead of aiming for success to aim for failure.

I called my parents that morning and asked them for the name of the rehab place. I typed it up on a computer, pulled up the web page, and saw pictures of people smiling, high-fiving, and swimming in a pool. The fact was I didn't know if I needed help. I didn't know if I had a problem. But seeing palm trees and people laughing looked pretty appealing considering that I woke up in my friend's car in snow and twenty-degree weather that morning.

In my delusional, twisted, misconstrued head, I thought I was entitled to go to Florida for treatment, that I needed a vacation. Because my life, which had consisted of partying, drinking, drugging, stealing, and sleeping, was so stressful and hard for poor old me that I needed to put my feet up in South Florida for a month or so.

In all reality, what would have benefitted me most was a trip to a local prison where I could be around people who had achieved what I was aspiring to achieve: being an outcast from society.

Within two hours I was on a plane to South Florida.

Chapter 6

"THEY TRIED TO MAKE ME GO TO REHAB"

NANCY

We had to move very quickly to get JP out of New York. Joe packed an overnight bag. He would accompany JP on the plane and fly back the next morning. I called the rehab center to tell them which flight JP would be arriving on. We arranged to meet JP in a parking lot at noon.

I wanted to say goodbye to our son. I wanted to somehow have some kind of meaningful interaction with him as he set off. That *Secret Belief* was still lurking in my heart. I thought maybe *this* would be the moment it happened. And he would tell me so as he left for rehab. And there would be a loving goodbye full of hugs.

Yeah, that was the script.

JP was sitting in a car when we got there—the same car that had served as his shelter for the last few days in the snowstorm. As JP rolled down the car window, the smell of marijuana blew into my face.

Great.

Gaunt and pale, JP looked at me with no expression. Just emptiness. His eyes were out of focus. Then without a word, he pushed the button to roll up the tinted car window. That was our goodbye.

A memory flashed through my mind from sixteen years before, when my father's body was in a casket at the funeral parlor after he died of a sudden heart attack. Just before the casket was closed, I leaned in to kiss my beloved father's face one last time. I expected to feel the warmth of my father's flesh on my lips as I had hundreds of times before. But my father's face was hard and cold as a stone. I always regretted giving Daddy that last kiss.

That's what came to my mind as I walked away from JP. Seeing my son so broken was like feeling my father's cold face on my lips. But instead of regretting that last image of JP, I was glad because it helped me to see clearly how dead he was.

After JP and Joe left, exhaustion hit hard. Annie announced we were going out for lunch. I enjoyed that meal with her because it was the first one I had really eaten since the police came to the house more than a week before. It was great to spend the time with Annie. I began to relax a little. My mind started to slow down.

Annie went back up to college later that afternoon. Grace and I watched a Disney movie together and ate grilled cheese sandwiches for dinner. That meal together was a tremendous gift, too. Molly arrived home. She had been at a friend's house visiting and had lots of funny stories to tell us. The house was calm. With JP in Florida in the safety net of a medical detox, predictability was restored. Joe called to let us know JP was met at the airport by a rehab employee and left immediately from there. Joe sounded very tired. He said he was enjoying the peace and quiet of watching TV in his hotel bedroom before his flight back in the morning.

Everyone was safe and sound. There was comfort knowing JP was getting help, and let's be completely honest—someplace where he was a plane ride away. I always tell parents whose kids are in rehab to take advantage of those twenty-eight days. It is a personal vacation for family members because it is a respite from the craziness of life with an active addict.

Late that night, a police car with its sirens on full blast sped by our house. The sound filled me with fear—and then I realized that *it was over*. The police weren't headed to our house. But for a very long time after, police sirens and flashing lights unpinned me. To this day, any kind of loud, emotionally charged situation sets off a chain reaction of anxiety for me that I must work hard to allay.

Resilience is hard work.

The next afternoon I was alone in the house. Joe hadn't gotten home yet. The phone rang with a Florida number I did not recognize. It was a call from JP from detox.

"I can't talk long. The nurse let me call from here. I don't have my phone," he said. "It's kind of like a hospital here. I just want you to know I need to be here. This is the right thing for me. I've got to go now, but I want you to know I am ok."

"I love you, JP," I said, crying and wishing I could figure out a way to stay longer on the phone and hear him sound so clearheaded.

"I love you, Mom."

After the call ended, I felt like a ten-ton weight had been lifted off my body. I held onto the hope of that conversation for a long, long time.

JP

For the next thirty days, I learned about all the different substances I had yet to use. I was able to glorify and revel in the dishonorable and unsuccessful life I was living. I achieved the coveted title of the coolest guy in rehab. I once again took something that could have been positive and for my good and, instead, used my demonic efforts to get the very least good out of it.

What I really needed was to pull my head out of my ass and make some major changes in my life and take positive sober action. But back then, even suggesting I take positive action or do something different with my life would have been like asking me to enter a seminary. It's a nice thought, but very far from ever actually happening.

When I try to explain how an addict's mind works, I jokingly say: it's the complete opposite of whatever you think. The scary part is there is a great deal of truth to that statement.

The average person who does not have any issues with

drugs or alcohol is guided by his or her conscience. In my experience, individuals with substance dependence may still have a conscience present, but that conscience does not come into play when they are making horrible choices. Even if there is a conscience, it's a quiet whisper blocked out by the monstrous screaming, banging, and chatter of their disease.

NANCY

We had little contact with JP. We spoke to his rehab counselor about once or twice a week. We tried to get on with our lives. It was amazingly good to just spend a simple, quiet night watching TV and then going to bed.

Call it gallows humor, but my daughters and I would sometimes joke around by singing the song, "Rehab."

> *"They tried to make me go to rehab*
> *I said, "No, no, no."*
> *Yes, I've been black*
> *But when I come back, you'll know, know, know,*
> *I ain't got the time*
> *And if my Daddy thinks I'm fine*
> *He's tried to make me go to rehab*
> *I won't go, go, go."*[3]

I thought it was a good sign that we could laugh about lyrics of a popular song nailing our family's awful experience so well. Of course, this was before Amy Winehouse died of alcohol poisoning. Now when I hear that song, I feel its deep sadness for a gifted life taken by addiction.

Those first weeks while JP was in Florida gave me the space to start the long process of sifting through the wreck-

---

3 Amy Winehouse, "Rehab," track 1 on Amy Winehouse, *Back to Black*, Island Records, 2006.

age, trying to answer that age-old question: *What the hell happened here?*

When a natural disaster strikes, teams of volunteers and trained professionals rush to the scene to mount a rescue effort. The world watches and waits as victims are pulled from the rubble and rejoices when they are found alive. But when the operation moves into a recovery effort, the sadness is palpable because everything possible has been done to save lives and now the search is on for the dead.

What had to happen in our family was the *exact opposite* of disaster management. Rescue mode—which is what enabling families do best—didn't work. This includes a fill-in-the-blanks array of behaviors families use in effort to rescue their addicted loved ones including, but not limited to: paying overdue bills; fixing cracked-up cars; buying new cars; hiring lawyers, tutors, and doctors; making excuses to bosses; providing shelter; and posting bail.

Ironically, these measures only ensure that the downward spiral will continue, ultimately leading to, as they say in 12-step programs: "death, jail, or an institution." For our family, recovery only began when the rescue campaign ended.

Easier said than done.

It has taken our family years of hard work, mistakes, good decisions, bad decisions, false starts, prayers, wizards, lousy counselors, and excellent ones to help us to make significant changes in our lives. It has taken all of this to finally get enough traction for the miracle of recovery to take place in God's time.

There was an administrator at Molly's school who knew what was going on with JP and the ripple effect—more like tsunami impact—it was having on our lives. She had raised a family of her own and was very kind to Molly. One day when I was at the school, she asked to me come into her office. She closed the door and shared that she had gone through a challenging time with her own teenager several years before. Her teen's behavior was not anywhere near the deep end of the pool that JP dove into. But she spoke with great compassion and said she believed that, ultimately, our family would find a way to a solution *"in God's time."*

She then hugged me and we each went on with our day.

In God's time.

At that moment, JP was in his new digs in rehab, and I was feeling a little more rested and thinking a little more clearly. The image of God as a divine timekeeper on the how, the when, and the where of our family's restoration was a comforting one. *In God's time* helped me to begin to reconnect with a deeper awareness of the flow of grace in our lives.

While I was studying in Oxford, England, during my sophomore year of college, my Uncle Luke, a gifted priest and college professor, wrote a letter to me about two Greek words used to describe the concept of time in the New Testament: chronos and kairos. Chronos is clock time. Everyday time. Time tethered to our mortality. Kairos time is God's time—eternal time. A divinely ordained time that cuts through the tick-tick-tick of the chronos clock.

John the Baptist declares at the start of Jesus' ministry: "The time has come. . . . The Kingdom of God has come near" (Mk 1:15). In that kick-off statement, John the Baptist was referring to a divinely ordained moment when heaven intersected with Earth to receive God's Son.

Kairos happens all around us. The divine breaks into the ordinary and feeds our faith. But in this situation, I was manacled to chronos time. Life was just a series of events cycling through every twenty-four hours.

In God's time.

Those words reminded me of what my Uncle Luke had explained so many years before in a letter written in his beautiful script. I needed to wake up my trust in God and remember there was *something* else going on here. The kairos of our existence was happening—even in the midst of the challenge. God's timing, God's presence, and God's benevolence were breaking into the chronos—whether I had eyes to see it or not.

Bottom line: JP was no longer calling the back seat of a car parked in the snow his home. He was safe, and he was getting help.

That had to be divine intervention.

The administrator's words were themselves some kai-ros—an appointed moment when kindness and lived wisdom shook some of the hopelessness out of me. I am indebted to that administrator for taking the risk of honestly sharing a part of her own life and faith at her workplace. Those three simple words she spoke have had great staying power with me over the years.

Chapter 7

THE SCHOOL OF DR. CIP

NANCY

I have replayed—far too many times—my role in what went wrong. It was a negative loop of sounds and images that wore a deep rut in my brain. At my worst, I thought of myself as an oven with a broken thermostat: there were many times in situations with JP that I did not hit the correct emotional temperature. I was lenient when I should have been tougher. I was tough about things I should have been easier about. I was inconsistent in situations requiring steadiness. And I was insistent about things that should have been shelved.

At times I sent out the wrong messages and signals to my son, and the scrambled form of communication left him without clear boundaries and a firm foundation upon which to formulate his own inner compass. And there were times I was angry and mouthy when things were going wrong. I carry deep regrets for all of it.

We sought a lot of help to get the message right. But the guide who helped us set our family on the most even course over the long haul was Dr. Bill Cipriano at St. Vincent's Hospital in Harrison, New York. We met him a little more than a year before JP went to rehab for the first time, and I can say without reservation that he has *never* steered us wrong.

In the lobby of St. Vincent's stands a large statue of St. Elizabeth Ann Seton with the words: "My Sisters and I Take Your Cause as Our Own." I felt hope when I first saw those words. It was only a flicker of hope, but even the tiny flame given off by a small, wooden match illuminates darkness. It was guidance from a saint whose help I sought when I was pregnant with Molly, and Joe and I were trying to find our way back to our Catholic faith.

St. Elizabeth was a wife, mother of five children, and the foundress of the Sisters of Charity. In 1991, I lit a candle at her shrine at St. Patrick's Cathedral shortly after getting out a hospital with a newly diagnosed heart arrhythmia found when I was fourteen weeks pregnant. I prayed to St. Elizabeth to safeguard Molly and to help us return to the Church. Both prayers were beautifully answered.

I believe she led us to a solution: the office of Dr. Cipriano.

Dr. Cipriano would have a good laugh if he heard me say a saint helped us find him. He looks like a Brooks Brothers version of Santa Claus: oxford cloth, man-tailored shirt with the sleeves rolled up, tie, khaki pants, red suspenders, a full white beard, and a mop of thick, white hair. He has a big, hearty laugh and a huge heart. He is very wise—stories and humor are his greatest tools for helping others.

A powerful combination.

JP arrived for the first appointment in a pissed-off mood.

"How can I help you today?" Dr. Cipriano asked.

"I don't need any of this shit," JP shot back and left, slamming the door.

I sat there feeling incredibly embarrassed, wondering what I should do. Dr. Cipriano never missed a beat.

"Well," he said, "I'll work with anyone who wants to work with me. Anyone who wants to do the work, I'll work with them."

His words began to put me at ease.

"I'll do the work," I replied with a surprising measure of composure in my voice.

And so began "the work" with Dr. Cipriano. I went to his office weekly, sometimes twice weekly. Joe came often too. As those weeks gathered into months, I began to understand what needed to be done to bring about change in our family.

"If what you are doing isn't working, don't keep doing it. Do the complete opposite," he told me.

Dr. Cipriano always delivers the truth with tremendous compassion. Over the years as we engaged various professionals in our search for a "solution," I found that many had lost their compassion. Maybe it was battle fatigue; maybe it was just their personal styles. But truth without compassion can feel awfully brutal. And then you are left trying to get over the brutality of the delivery, when what you really need to be doing is wrestling with the challenge posed by the truth. Either way, Dr. Cipriano's concern for our family always came through.

Bit by bit, he helped me unclench my grasp on what wasn't working to reach out and grab hold of a new way of doing things that would work. He helped us prepare for getting JP out of our house and into rehab. Then he guided us to the next step of our family's recovery process: JP could not come home when the twenty-eight-day treatment was finished.

"You will know he is serious about his recovery if he agrees to stay down in Florida for aftercare in a halfway house. If he insists on coming home, then he is not serious about working a recovery program and is headed for a relapse. Then you have to bar the doors and windows again."

What I wanted more than *anything* was to get the time back with my family. I wanted us all to be happy together at home, as we had been years before.

Clearly, that wasn't happening.

Dr. Cipriano was direct: there would be no reclaiming time.

"Forget about it. It's gone," he said. "You're never going to get that time back. You are on new ground now. You will make new memories in time. But you can't get back those years. So stop trying.

Let him go. Live your own life with your girls and Joe. JP's got to live his own life now."

Chapter 8

PENANCE AND A BADASS DUDE

NANCY

There was no getting around the truth that JP needed a relocation plan after rehab.

The counselors working with JP in Florida explained that there were lots of halfway houses where JP could begin to build a new life. The thought of our nineteen-year-old son living in a halfway house was unsettling. I had absolutely no idea how halfway houses worked. My fearful mind envisioned a rundown building loaded with toothless, unshaven, old men in dirty clothes sitting around a table in a dark room with no future ahead of them.

I didn't want any such thing for my son, but what was left in New York for him? Another back seat of a car to call home?

Five days before JP's discharge date, Joe and I went down to participate in the rehab's family program. Before leaving, I wanted to clean house spiritually through the Sacrament of Penance. Our parish priest, Father Andrew, was a family friend. He understood the strain this challenge had placed on our marriage. As part of the Sacrament of Penance, I discussed with Father Andrew how I felt I had failed my family, Joe in particular, with my outbursts of anger and frustration. I told him I felt I had failed JP as a parent.

Father Andrew did not judge me. He listened with kindness and patience. And when it was time for him to give a penance, he taught me a lesson I have never forgotten.

"Nancy, how much time will you be in seminars for?"

"From 8:30 to 2:30."

"How much time will you spend with JP?"

"From 2:30 to 4," I said, wondering where Father Andrew was going with these scheduling questions.

"OK. Do the work you have to do. Spend the time you are allowed with JP. But at four o'clock every day, I want you to put this all aside and focus on you and Joe. Go for walks on the beach, laugh, eat great dinners together. Get some sleep. Have some fun. See this as a vacation. You two deserve this time together.

"Use it for your best advantage. I don't know how you both have gone through all you have. Enjoy the gift of this time. The girls will be fine. JP is where he needs to be. *Be with Joe.* That's your penance."

I looked at Father Andrew in amazement. He had identified something incredibly profound. Joe and I had spent loads of time trying to put out fires in our family. And that was the right thing to do. We were the parents of a large family with many needs. But what had we done for each other in all that time? You can't pour from an empty cup. We needed some down time together—even if it had to be carved into a trip for a rehab family program! I hugged Father Andrew and stepped out of the Parish House into the crisp March evening air, renewed by the sacrament of Penance and the prospect of using this time in Florida as a positive with the most important person in my life—my wonderful husband, Joe.

We participated in the program for six hours a day. It was time well spent. JP looked a lot healthier. He had gained weight, and he smiled easily. He was happy to see us and asked a lot of questions about how things were at home.

We were glad to see JP, but we also took Father Andrew's words to heart. Joe and I enjoyed our lunch breaks together. We went out for dinner every night. We took walks on the beach at sunset and even won $500 on a scratch-off lottery ticket.

Still hanging over our heads was the issue of JP's reentry into the world on Day 28. We knew less than a month of treatment would not qualify as a permanent game changer.

On the third day of the family seminars, we could drive him back to rehab—a ten-minute trip.

We swung through a hamburger drive-thru to get him some food. He thanked us profusely for stopping to get him a bagful of greasy burgers and fries.

"I want to come home," he blurted out. "I want to be with the family. I know what I have to do, and I can do it at home."

JP deeply felt the pull to be home and really believed he could maintain his new sobriety there. But we received good counsel from Bill, who ran the family program and was well experienced with families in recovery. He is the quintessential southern gentleman, impeccably dressed in well-pressed pants, a tailored gingham shirt, and highly polished brown leather loafers.

In a Southern drawl, he coached us on what to say to JP.

"Sometimes you just gotta say: 'No son. That's just not how it's gonna be.'"

Bill told us to check out area halfway houses. He gave us the names and addresses of a few places to visit, including one run by a friend.

"Paul does a good job with those boys. Go take a drive down and look at his place."

I was feeling pretty good—even a bit optimistic—about things when we went to visit the halfway houses. The first two were apartment buildings in gated developments. The rooms were clean and nicely painted, with new furniture and patios. The managers were well spoken and readily answered our questions about life at a halfway house and the rules JP would be required to follow. My fears about huddles of toothless men were beginning to fade—and we still had our appointment to visit Healing Properties managed by Bill's friend Paul.

Based on our knowledge of Bill—a well-mannered, southern gentleman, I had an image of what Healing House and Paul, whom he spoke of so highly, would be like. I pictured Paul as a younger version of Bill—preppy clothes and a polite manner. I pictured Healing House as an Old Florida-style place in a nice section of town with pots of red geraniums flourishing on a front porch. I pictured Paul holding house meetings in a sunny living room with comfortable armchairs and a table holding a tray of Arnold Palmers and cookies for refreshments. I pictured the residents as young men well on the road to sobriety, who on their days off from work or school spent time surfing or playing tennis in the nearby town courts.

Then Joe drove along a very down-on-its-luck street.

This is Healing House?

Standing around the weed-lined driveway that looked like a parking lot for last-gasp cars and motorcycles were unshaven young guys with all manner of tattoos, in tee shirts or no shirts and smoking cigarettes. The house part of Healing House was a motley grouping of bungalow buildings, just this side of shacks, painted an absurd shade of electric blue and held together with old wood and even older roof shingles. It looked like a strong wind would flatten them in an instant.

So much for the potted geraniums.

Joe and I looked at each other in disbelief.

What the hell is this?

I wanted to throw the car in reverse and get out of this place clearly on the verge of having a condemned sign staked in front of it. But I knew enough—just barely enough—to trust Bill directing us to this ramshackle collection of buildings for a good reason.

We asked the young men standing around where we could find Paul. They pointed to a door; we knocked and stepped into a dark, smelly room that looked as if it had not seen a paintbrush or a breath of fresh air in decades.

In walked Paul. Shaved head, a beard, a sleeve of tattoos, a leather band around one wrist and spiked band on the other.

Badass biker guy in recovery with an attitude.

And I could read volumes with his first look at me in a pink-and-green sundress, pink-and-green sandals, and a handbag to match.

Clueless suburban mom with an addicted son.

It was a great start for both of us.

Paul led us quickly through the warren of rooms. We looked at the back of his shaved head the entire time. He never turned around to talk to us. He simply stated each room's function: kitchen, bunk room, living room. They were all so dark that it was hard to distinguish one from the other.

I tried to ask him a question about what the residents did for meals.

"Ramen noodles."

"Ramen noodles?"

"Yeah, they eat a lot of Ramen noodles around here."

Okaaaay.

When we got back outside after the three-minute tour, I asked the back of Paul's head what he attributed the success of his work with the young men in recovery to. After all, Bill had told us he did a "good job with those boys."

This time he did turn around to look at us—for a second.

"God and AA," he barked without a flicker of a smile. "God and AA."

I had reached my limit with the staccato, back-of-the-head exchanges with this guy, Paul. I felt in my heart there was a reason we were standing in this run-down place. But Paul was so incredibly unfriendly and, frankly, hardheaded, I was done. It was time for a little sober self- disclosure to at least temper the level of cluelessness Paul was attributing to me.

Most importantly, we needed to get to the heart of whether this place would be a good fit for JP. So, as Paul turned around again, I said brightly to the back of his head: "God and AA? Really? That's great. That's all you really need. I've learned that a day at a time for myself for the last eighteen years."

Now *that* got Paul's attention.

"You're eighteen years sober?" he asked, looking directly at me.

"Yes. It will be nineteen years in July with God's help."

And with that, something softened in Paul's voice and his stance.

"That's really great."

"It's what I want for my son."

We looked at each other silently for a moment or two. Joe saw it happen. A connection was made.

He gestured over to a bunch of guys standing around a bike.

"Those guys came through. When they got out of rehab, they didn't go home. They stayed down here and worked at it. They lived in halfway houses with me for a while. They got jobs. They went through the Steps. Now they have their own apartments and are back in school. It takes time. It can happen."

Joe extended his hand to Paul and told him we would bring JP back the next day. We started walking toward our rental car —a Geo the color of a fluorescent pumpkin.

"Hey Paul!" I called. "How do you like our sick whip?"

He laughed and shook his head.

As Humphrey Bogart said in final scene of *Casablanca*: "This is the beginning of a beautiful friendship."

If it were a beauty contest, Healing House would have been thrown out in the first round. But I *knew* Paul could teach JP something about sobriety.

The next day we brought JP to all the halfway houses. Quite uncharacteristically, I said only one thing about the choices.

"Healing House is not a pretty place, but I know you will like this guy Paul. He has good sobriety and a great sense of humor."

JP

I pulled up to a run-down, blue halfway house and saw a bunch of kids huddled around, smoking cigarettes, standing next to a bald guy with tattoos. I was introduced to this individual, whose name was Paul.

I said hi to him.

He replied, "Wow, look at that hair, dude," and dusted his hand through my hair.

I wasn't sure what he meant, but I knew he wasn't being genuine and giving me a compliment. It was kind of like when you are standing next to two people speaking a language you don't understand. You can tell they are making fun of you; you can sense nonverbally that something is being said about you that isn't very good, but you don't really know what it is.

I replied to Paul, "This is New York hair. You guys probably wouldn't know about it down here."

He replied, "Yeah man, look at that hairdo, dude. That is serious. Wow, man."

I then said:" So, where's the tour?" because every time he replied I seemed to be getting more offended and angrier.

And I had a feeling that if I punched this guy in the face, my residency at this shanty halfway house wouldn't happen.

NANCY

JP's arguments against going to any halfway house began to escalate in the car on the return trip to the treatment center. Armed with the coaching we received from Dr. Cipriano and Bill, we were ready.

"You are getting out of rehab in three days, JP. Mom and I are leaving here tomorrow," Joe said in an even voice. "You can't come home. That is not an option. If you go back to New York, we will continue to press the charges we brought against you last month. It would be in your best interest to choose one of these places to live and continue with your recovery."

We all sat in the car in silence.

I began to pray hard and fast.

"Please, God, let this work out. Please get through to him. I do not have it in me to endure another ugly showdown. I don't want to go through him homeless again. Please help this situation. I give it to you."

JP had little to say when he got out of the car. Early sobriety is an emotional roller coaster because the person is experiencing life without the numbing medication of a substance. And if JP was in the first seat on the roller coaster as it took a nosedive, I still felt like I was right there next to him because I wanted so badly for things to work and for him to get the program. That is why I have always loved the slogan: "Life on life's terms," because it gets to the heart of the need to live the life you are given. It means accepting circumstances as they are right in front of you. That afternoon, it meant living with the uncertainty of JP's choice of a next move.

Bill's parting words were good counsel.

"The ball is in his court now. You've done all you can do. Let it go. Trust the process."

On our last night in Florida, Joe and I had dinner and went to the beach. It was just past sunset and thick clouds scudded across the dark sky. The wind was blowing hard, and the surf was dark and rough. We walked along the shore holding hands and talked. There were still many uncertainties. And there would be for a long time. But we agreed the trip had been a good one on many levels.

Heading back to the car, Joe's cell phone rang. It was JP.

"I'll go to Healing House."

JP

After getting out of treatment, I felt—with thirty days of questionable sobriety—that I now had the knowledge to make life-changing decisions for myself. What I really needed to do was to pull my head out of my ass and take suggestions from people who actually had solid sobriety.

If I had done that then, I would have saved myself and anyone who came in close vicinity of me a lot of pain and heartache.

In my mind, the clinicians and professionals did not know what was best for me. The people who had done this for their living, gone to school, and had experience in the field of addiction counseling informed me that I had a bad drug habit and that I needed to continue to seek help for myself.

I did not want to listen.

My parents flew down and informed me that there was still no place at home for me, which was a brilliant decision on their end. If I had to place myself in their shoes, I would not have even flown down to visit myself. Their decision to divert the typhoon of destruction that I caused at home to

South Florida probably saved them both a few years on their lives. I, once again, was resistant to the help I needed to get.

If the scenario had been different, and a professional who specialized in cancer treatment told me I was afflicted with that disease and if I didn't seek a continuum of treatment, I would die, there would have been no question or the need to force my hand to continue treatment. The fact is, drug addiction and alcoholism centers in one's thinking and distorts rational thoughts. My parents' ultimatum left me with no choice but to agree to begin living at a halfway house.

Chapter 9

GOLDFISH AND DISNEY WORLD

NANCY

So, while JP was in South Florida fresh out of rehab, we all put our efforts into living our lives at home in New York. We had been immersed in so much commotion that Joe and I rarely went out. We knew we had to push ourselves to get back to some semblance of the regular rhythms of life.

My brother, Jim, and his wife, Tara, knew we needed some help with this. They began to invite us to their home every Sunday evening for a family supper. Those evenings together were a good starting point for us to reconfigure ourselves as a family. It's amazing how something as simple as a home-cooked Sunday supper can feed the soul. Those meals sure did. Tara is a great cook. Jim, eighteen months younger than I, is my Irish twin. The two of them cared tremendously about our family and didn't judge our situation. They just believed in us, JP included, and in our ability to get to a better place.

We felt safe and accepted there. Those Sunday evenings were a time when we were living in the solution—not the problem. Gathered at their long, wooden table with their three children and our daughters, reciting grace together, sharing old stories and jokes, and eating delicious food helped us to feel that we were still a vibrant, loving family.

Yes, a little banged up, but vibrant and loving just the same.

As things unraveled, I distanced myself from some people because I sensed that while they believed they were being well meaning and helpful, there was judgment and finger-wagging going on. Over time I developed a theory on challenges and the support of the larger community. There are challenges that rally family and friends to reach out in support. Cards are sent, and flowers and home-cooked meals are brought to the home.

An addiction crisis can be isolating. No one comes to your door with a casserole dish or bouquet the day after the police arrive at your home. Very few people call to see how your family is holding up while your son or daughter is in medical detox. The majority want to respect a family's privacy and are probably at a loss for the right words to say. But there are those who view the struggling addict and family as a caricature of compound failure and sin.

During the years I felt so cut off, it was mainly because my own shame and fear built a wall between me and others. There were many good people who tried to reach out. But there also were times I had to guard myself and my family against judgment.

All of this helped me understand something about how Jesus walked the Earth. Jesus did not associate much with those whose lives had the perfect appearance of a magazine cover. He didn't have a lot of time to get his work done, and his work had to do with *a bunch of really sketchy characters*: adulterers, tax collectors, lepers, prostitutes, sinners, and the demon-possessed. Jesus ate with them, healed them, counseled them, and laughed and wept with them, too.

If Jesus showed up today, he would probably not stay very long in our beautiful churches with congregations who seem to have it all together. I think he would pull up a chair in a church basement, holding meetings for those who were lost and are now truly found. He would be wherever the hurting and marginalized gather and probably stay the hell away from *holier-than-thou-ness*. Christ's miracles took place in the lives of broken people. The ones who were healed always recognized that, yes indeed, they absolutely needed Christ's presence. Their need helped make the leap of faith happen between what Christ was giving and their getting it.

My backup on this is a Jesuit priest who is also a very good friend. Time and again, Father Mark reminds me about how Jesus can be found in the midst of a mess.

"Nancy, if we expect to have it all together before we invite Jesus in, it will never happen. He comes into the messiness of our lives. Jesus doesn't come to meet us in our perfection. He comes to meet us in our brokenness."

Father Mark's words were a comfort when I felt the sting of the tongue-waggers and finger-pointers. I began to realize that just as Jesus had boundless compassion for those struggling in the gospel stories, he had boundless compassion for our family. It was the beginning of understanding that there was a message in our mess.

Damn good stuff.

Meanwhile, JP was down in Florida trying to muscle through. I didn't know if he was trying very hard. I wanted to believe the best and that it was all to work out—quickly. He needed to find a job. He needed to use public transportation. He needed to go to 12-step meetings daily. He needed to find a way to finish high school. He needed a lot of things, and he was struggling with most of them.

He was wrestling with the demons of early sobriety—living life without self-medication, dramas, and destruction. Difficult for him to do, and difficult for us to watch him struggle and not rush in to help.

During those early weeks, Molly celebrated her sixteenth birthday with a big party in our backyard. Molly wanted a party that included everyone she loves—not only school friends but longtime family friends, who had watched her grow up. The celebration had this wonderful intergenerational feel to it. We wanted to make it a memorable night for her. Molly had one request: instead of flowers at each table, she asked for bowls of goldfish.

Goldfish, Molly? How about some pretty roses?

When we went to buy the destined-to-be-centerpiece goldfish, we had to solemnly promise the pet store manager that no partygoer would swallow them. We have a little goldfish pool in our yard, so we assured the manager that the fish would have a lovely new home after the party was over. There was something very comical about keeping more than sixty goldfish alive in big metal pots filled with sloshing, cold water the night before the party. The water had to be changed every three hours so the fish wouldn't die. With all the water changes, temperature checks, scooping fish in nets, and mopping up spills, I felt like I was an employee at a seaquarium.

But we managed to keep those fish alive with a lot of laughter. We love to say the Vericker family puts the fun in dys*fun*ctional. It's become a family slogan of sorts. All the party preparations felt good to do together because we were back to celebrating something important in the life of our family.

The party took place on a gorgeous May evening. Molly wore a colorful, summery dress and a silver crown on her head—after all she was Good Golly Miss Molly, *the* Birthday Girl. During the party, she had a candle-lighting ceremony where she dedicated each one of sixteen candles to a loved one. Molly stood before seventy guests and paid tribute to her brother with a candle.

"This candle is for JP," she said. "I wish he could be here tonight, but he couldn't. He is taking care of himself right now, and I am proud of him for doing that. My brother and I would always pull pranks when we were little. I always called him My King. He always makes me laugh. I really love him, and I miss him."

Everyone was touched by her loving words. It was a good night.

As the weeks went by, we spoke to Paul often, as he was supervising JP's life at Healing House. Paul never sugarcoats anything. While I was worrying that JP was depressed, Paul told us JP needed to work harder: to find employment and to pray more.

In the early part of the summer, Paul said it would be a good time for us to visit. It had been more than four months since we had seen our son. We decided we would all go to Disney World as part of the trip: it wasn't a big party scene, and it appealed to the very wide range of ages that comprised our family.

JP and I found a meeting to attend near the hotel. JP picked up a coin marking six months of sobriety. It was wonderful to be there to see it happen. As a family, we went on rides, took pictures and swam in the pool. We went to Mass. I felt deeply grateful to be sitting with my children and my husband in church. JP leaned over to me during the Mass and whispered:

"I am the Prodigal Son come home, Mom."

"I know, Manz."

We began to feel hope again. The dread I had lived with for months was gone.

It didn't last very long.

Three weeks later, JP's mood plummeted. He told us he was having a hard time finding a job, and he was struggling with anxiety. We knew a key to his continued progress was employment and attendance at meetings. I was still optimistic that he wanted to stay sober. I was worried he was slipping into depression and wanted to have him see a medical doctor.

But when we spoke to Paul, we heard a different take. His candor, experience, and humor cut through our entrenched thinking. It went to the heart of a 12-step slogan: "Nothing changes if nothing changes."

Families in the throes of addiction close themselves off to the outside, functioning world. Fear, shame and a good measure of know-it-all-ism bolster the walls of this closed-off family system. These families, and we were one of them, are intent on just getting through the struggle of living day-to-day with an unpredictable and destructive force. It is very difficult to allow new voices carrying the message of new ways of living—and ultimately, healing—in.

It takes a guide with great heart and skill to penetrate these walls and help lead a family to what Bill W. called "the Road of Happy Destiny." Once JP landed in Florida, Paul became that guide and his presence in all our lives was a source of healing for our family. We trusted Paul. We listened to him. We took his suggestions. Paul told Joe and me it was time for us to stop paying JP's halfway house rent and to hold his feet to the fire to get and keep a job.

"He needs to pray more," Paul said. "And, excuse my language, he needs to get his lazy ass in gear and seriously look for a job. He's not doing that. That's why he feels lousy because he is taking his will back. He wants to do things his own way, and he is not doing what he is supposed *to be doing*."

JP

For the next six months, I saw other guys whom I had become close to make the transformation from feeling hopeless, like I did, to living productive lives. I saw them start carving their way into life, and building a foundation for a happy life. At the time, I didn't really understand why that wasn't happening for me.

I wasn't sure, but I didn't think it had anything to do with the fact that I was not working, the fact that I was still behaving the same way I did when I was on drugs, and the fact that I still did not take any simple suggestions that were gently offered to me—which consisted of going to meetings and getting a sponsor.

To me, it just seemed like too much of a hassle, and again I seemed to think that I knew best what was best for me. In my mind, this happiness and creation of a new life, which I saw others getting, was just going to fall right into my lap. All I needed to do was to sleep twelve hours a day, smoke cigarettes, and continue to manipulate my family.

The only things I responded to with some sort of half-assed action were extremes. When I was faced with an extreme ultimatum or impending doom, I would then decide to put forth minimal effort to avoid consequences. These ultimatums were given to me by Paul, who was my friend and the owner of the halfway house.

Paul told me, "Look kiddo, you gotta get up off your goddamned lazy ass and get a job."

I then fed him a line of bullshit listing an array of half measures I had made. I was put on notice by the house manager that I had one week to find a job, otherwise I could no longer live at the halfway house. I was so full of shit I believed my own lies about why I wasn't getting anything done.

But with that ultimatum pending, I made a few simple phone calls.

And what do you know? Within forty-eight hours I was gainfully employed.

NANCY

JP launched a campaign for us to buy him a car. He argued it would be easier to get a job if he did not have to rely on limited public transportation. It was an accurate measure of how I was still so easily bamboozled by him that I began to think he was right. I asked Paul his thoughts. He told me absolutely not— JP needed to struggle. Well, that took care of my feeling sorry for my son.

"No, Son. That's just not how it's gonna be."

JP began a series of jobs, each lasting only a week or so. He was losing traction, and we were losing patience.

Chapter 10

"IT'S UP TO YOU, NEW YORK, NEW YORK"

JP

I got a job at a phone room, selling cruise packages. All the other stellar employees there were mostly ex-convicts, living just on the outskirts of staying sober—if that. After taking the bus for a week and working there, I felt I deserved a reward—to get high. In my mind, I believed my life was *so* hard and my career of one week was *so* stressful, it was time for a reward.

That night I picked up a bag of weed from someone at work. I waited till everyone in the halfway house was asleep and went outside and smoked. I remember thinking as the weed kicked in how badly I had missed that feeling. I sat with headphones on listening to music, songs I was very familiar with but because I was high it was like a whole new experience. I felt like my imagination was bursting and there were rainbows coming out of my head.

The following day, I decided to pick up a bag of pot again and added some prescription medication to my purchase. Looking back, I realize this was my addicted mind in overdrive. The decision to throw pills in the mix was made somewhere in the back of my mind before I even bought the first bag of pot. The inevitability of this relapse was caused by me not taking any positive action to behave as a grown, responsible, sober man.

That night I took the pills and smoked the pot and once

again fell in love with the feeling. I was numb from all the pain and heartache I had in my core, which was made up of feeling distant from and rejected by my family, being the black sheep of the family, ruining my relationship with my former girlfriend, stealing, and lying. I could list all the pain and heartache I felt for the next twelve pages, but you get the idea.

When I was high I didn't have to look at that shit. I got high because it made me feel *normal*. The nightly routine I was doing with drugs quickly became a daily routine. I was now high before I even got to work. I realized I was going to fail the drug test given at the halfway house. Instead of doing what most people logically would do—stop getting high and ask for help—I figured it would be smarter to run.

I started saving 90 percent of every paycheck, so I could do just that.

Three weeks later, I was preparing my doses in the bathroom for that night. I was already inebriated, and I must have dropped a pill or a fragment of a pill on the floor. The next day I was at work for about an hour and received a call telling me to be ready to take a drug test when I got home.

Guess what happened next?

I went back to the halfway house and started packing my bags because I knew my backup plan would have to kick in a lot sooner than I expected. The following morning, I went and bought a one-way Greyhound bus ticket back to New York City. I began calling my old connections in New York, telling them I would be coming home.

NANCY

Just before Labor Day the phone call came from Paul: JP had relapsed and was living in a flophouse with two other relapsed young men he had met at the halfway house.

"He won't last long there," Paul assured us. "There is no electricity in the place. He'll come back and start over again."

JP wasn't answering his phone. The panic that had disappeared for a few months came back hard and fast.

We heard from him the last week of August.

"Yeah, I'm coming home. I'm taking a bus. I'll be home in two weeks."

"You'll have no money. You'll have no place to live. We will reinstate the charges against you in court."

"Yeah, of course you will, because you want to make me miserable. I'll see you in two weeks."

JP had been in South Florida for seven months.

The anxious, angry, indecisive, isolated, and tearful me was also back in the building, replacing the woman who had begun to emerge from the wreckage. Despite our threats, I knew JP was hell-bent on coming back.

But there was a sliver of sanity still in me from the seven-month respite. I decided that for the remaining few weeks before he came home, I was going to enjoy life. I acted as if his arrival wasn't imminent, and I tried to shake off the fear growing by leaps and bounds in my heart. Annie, Molly, and Grace were starting back to school. I had a deadline from Fordham to complete my master's thesis before December. Joe was busy with his work.

There were plenty of good and productive things going on with the rest of our family. At that moment, JP was some distant, offshore hurricane swirling in the warm southern waters. It was time for us to enjoy the nice weather before the storm hit.

One week went by. Then two. And then three.

Joe and I started to believe that *maybe, just maybe,* JP had a change of heart. I kind of tiptoed around hoping that he would decide to stay in Florida and receive help. We didn't really know where he was living or what he was doing. Paul kept in touch with us and told us he was trying to talk JP out of coming home.

And then one afternoon at the end of September, Paul called again.

"Nancy, I heard he got on a bus to New York yesterday. You keep in touch with me when he gets home. You can call me any time; you know that. He will hit another bottom and when he does, he'll come back to Florida; I guarantee it."

I thanked Paul, then immediately called Joe and started to cry.

"It's over. He's coming back to New York."

JP

The trip on the bus to New York took almost four days. It was horrible. But in keeping with the theme of my life at the time, it was a *perfect* fit. Sitting on the beat-up bus with the team of reject passengers arguing with each other, crying babies with smelly diapers, flies, and uncomfortable seats really blended into the mud-colored paint of my life at the time.

The bus stopped off in probably every single one of the top-ranked worst cities in America. At a stop in one of the seediest parts of Orlando, I saw an individual who met all criteria as a drug dealer. I bought a pill off him, thinking it was an Oxycodone, and got back on the bus, looked at it, and knew it wasn't.

But I wanted so badly to feel high again for the rest of the trip that, even knowing it was not real, I took it anyway.

I still to this day don't know what I took.

A friend picked me up from the Port Authority in New York City. This geographic change made me feel temporarily better about the shambles my life was in.

I got a room at a crack motel I used to frequent. Everyone I had used with and partied with turned out to celebrate my return. It felt good to get high, but inside, even with all the fog in my mind from drugs, I knew this was fucked up. I had probably $500 to my name and not many resources and outlets to get more money.

The next three weeks were filled with very heavy drug use, fights, scams, more heavy drug use, and misery. I now had successfully spent all the money I had saved on drugs and crack hotels. I lost probably fifteen pounds in that three-week period.

I remember thinking way in the back of my mind: "This is probably going to end badly."

And my gut was *always* right.

NANCY

We didn't know when JP arrived in New York. We didn't know his whereabouts. It sounds awful, but it was better that way. He finally called us on Columbus Day.

"Yeah, I'm in a place in Yonkers. I want to see you."

Joe and I had decided we would make good on our decision to reactivate the charges against him. We hoped the prospect of a court case would be incentive for JP to decide to return to Florida and treatment. But that was not our son's game plan.

We met JP at a diner to set some ground rules: the order of protection remained in effect and the court case would go forward. We offered him a plane ticket back to Florida.

Our meeting did not end well.

JP

At that point, this is what I believed my life would consist of: I was destined to use drugs, sell drugs, lie, cheat, and steal.

I was now faced with a dilemma. I had no more money and nowhere to sleep. My parents were not allowing me to live back at home. A friend said I could stay the night at his house. I told his mother my sob story when I got there. The next morning, I was woken up by this mother, who was hysterical and angry.

I didn't really remember much from the night before. But they had security cameras in front of and inside their house, so I was able to piece together what happened. The mom had a full bottle of prescribed Xanax, which her son and I demolished. What the mom saw on the security camera from the night before was me continuously trying to get up the stairs and falling down each time. I was then carried up the stairs by her son.

After being told to leave their house, I called another friend, who quickly picked me up. I then began the daily activity of somehow getting drugs and using drugs all day and all night. The restraining order was still in effect.

And I really had nowhere to go.

NANCY

Another two weeks went by before we heard from JP. He was living in a run-down motel. He asked me to meet him at a local McDonalds, where we used to go for breakfast when he was in nursery school. It had a ball jump where, years before, JP and Molly had loved to whoop it up together. I sat there remembering all the hopes I had for his future when he was four years old.

"I've run out of money and I need a place to live."

"We can't help you. I've got a thesis to finish. Go back to Florida. Go to meetings. Talk to Paul."

"I need an apartment."

"Your case is due in court next week, JP. We can't help you as long as you are in New York."

Fordham's deadline was a good thing. It kept me going when JP was homeless and back in court. At one point, I seriously considered not completing the thesis. I didn't think I could gather my thoughts to write anything coherent. But in his wise, Jesuit way, Father Mark, my classmate at Fordham, reasoned that quitting would be a terrible loss to me, and to Joe, who had given his unconditional support. And, he asked, what kind of example would it be to my daughters if I didn't finish?

Throughout those weeks, JP was required to appear in court and I went. I sat in the back of the courtroom on the opposite side of the aisle from our son. We didn't speak at all. He barely made eye contact with me and would walk out without any acknowledgment.

Looking back, my going there was a big mistake. I didn't extricate myself, let the case run its course, and get on with what I had to do. It was painful and humiliating to watch. I thought I was being a good mother by showing up. It was unnecessary and a poor choice. Dr. Cipriano told me so.

"Why do you go there? The court can handle JP without you being in the room."

The stuck part of me couldn't wrap my mind around the idea of not showing up.

The stuck and muleheaded part of me.

JP had a well-qualified, court-assigned lawyer represent-ing him. We had nothing to do with that. My decision to sit there week after week extended the emotional toll. On some level, I felt JP needed protecting. I had the whole scenario backward.

Judge Patrick assigned JP to outpatient drug evaluation and treatment, which he blew off. At the next court date, the judge told JP he would be heading to jail for failing to comply with the court order. I knew Judge Patrick meant business. JP's attorney asked for one more chance, which the judge reluctantly granted.

By then JP had been in New York for almost two months. He was homeless. He was jobless. He was spiraling down-ward. The Insomnia Club was back in business as Joe and I were sleepless every night, expecting some terrible phone call about JP.

The only hopeful moments came every few weeks when Paul would call.

"Hey! How's the Vericker family doing?" he'd cheerily ask.

During every conversation, Paul would tell me it was a *great thing* JP's life was falling apart because it would bring him closer to his bottom. The rational part of me knew Paul was completely correct. The crazed mother part of me did not. Paul kept encouraging us.

"He'll come back. He'll leave New York and come back down here to get sober. I promise."

I clung to Paul's words, but it seemed a long way off.

JP

I asked my parents to meet me at a local diner. They did. During dinner I explained I was not a drug dealer or an alco-holic, that I just had a rough patch and it was now over. I had a job as a waiter. I told them I was only drinking, and I was managing that. I convinced them to help me get into the Y to live.

The room at the Y was probably fifty square feet.

NANCY

Just before Thanksgiving, JP called to tell us he had a job working nights at a restaurant. He sounded better and asked if we would be willing to help him get a room at the YMCA, down the street from the new job.

We knew he was desperate, if he was suggesting the Y. The *last time* he lived at the Y, after failing out of high school, he vowed he would rather die than ever go back there again. We were right back to where we had all been before: with JP living at the Y waiting for the trapdoor of his life to open again.

THE
BACK
STORY

Chapter 11

"CHAIN, CHAIN, CHAIN"

NANCY

In 1990, I began attending a 12-step meeting on Wednesday evenings in a basement classroom of a church school. It was a beginners meeting, which means it was geared to people with under a year of sobriety. About fifty people packed into that small room, wrapped in a haze of cigarette smoke—because back then you could still smoke in a meeting. Three-quarters of the seats were filled with guys—every one of them with a war story of how he finally landed with a thud in a Catholic school basement classroom—to learn the ropes of how not to pick up the first drink.

This meeting had two leaders: someone with just over a year of sobriety and someone with what's known in 12-step lexicon as "time." The meeting attendees jammed into that room each week because the leaders, Brian, the elder statesmen, and Gwen, the newbie, were great speakers, delivering the message of sobriety with humor, insight, and directness. I chose to go to that meeting because it was convenient. I stayed because it was a place where I truly learned the fundamentals and made a lifelong friend in Brian.

The first time, I felt intimidated by all the smoke and all the guys. I was a thirty-four-year-old wife and mother of two young children. I hadn't crashed a car, been arrested, filed for bankruptcy, stolen money, served time in jail, lost friends, wrecked my marriage, or lost custody of my children in a court battle. In 12-step parlance, those were my *yets*—as in that hadn't happened *yet*.

But for the grace of God, there go I.

I was in pain, knew my family history with the disease, and knew that despite how it appeared, I was beginning to develop an emotional and physical dependence on alcohol to take the edge off at night after I put my babies to bed. I was in control, but it was there lurking in the shadows. When I was in college, running around with friends, I sometimes blacked out when I drank—a big red flag to a looming problem. I did not drink like a college girl once I met my husband and we began dating. But I knew that very often when I had a drink—even just a glass of wine—whether it was at a party or with a meal, the result would often be a crashing hangover and ultimately such a jangled emotional state that I would get into an argument with my husband.

RID—restless, irritable, and discontent—is an apt description of the alcoholic. And *that* was a pretty spot-on description of me back then.

There was a solid family history of alcoholism in my family tree: my maternal grandfather, Frank, died an incurable alcoholic. My grandmother Mary—known as Mom-Mom—threw Frank out of the house when my mother was a toddler after she discovered he was stealing money from my mother's little piggy bank. This was at the height of the Depression, and Mom-Mom then became a single parent, responsible for supporting my mother on her own. She scrambled hard to do that, working as a cook in a nursery school, teaching typing in night school, and one winter resorting to chopping up rafters in the attic to heat the very modest home they shared with my great-grandmother during those lean years.

Many years later, my grandmother met and married Walter King, the man I knew as my grandfather Pop-Pop. He was an intelligent, soft-spoken, hardworking man who was several years younger than my grandmother. Born a Baptist, he converted to Catholicism after marrying Mom-Mom. Theirs was a happy union, bringing great stability and committed love to the lives of my grandmother, my mother, and the daughter she and Pop-Pop had together, my aunt Mary Rose.

My mother told me that when she was growing up, she often had to visit her father in the neighborhood bar. It was what my mother and grandmother never said about Frank that made me know his alcoholism was a heartache for them both. The most I ever learned was when I was twenty-five years old, visiting my grandparents at a tiny beach cottage way out at the tip of the Long Island coast. I loved visiting my grandparents. I treasured Pop-Pop's quiet thoughtfulness. And I adored Mom-Mom. She was always a strong, nurturing, loving presence in my life. One afternoon a dense gray fog blew in from the Sound. Mom-Mom and I went out for a walk on the beach in advance of the coming storm. Afterward, we sat next to each other on rickety wooden steps leading to the beach that was enveloped in the mist. My grandmother stared at the swirl of fog and ocean mist and in a very soft voice began to speak of events that had happened fifty years before, when she was married to Frank. I don't know what prompted my grandmother to share those stories. I've always thought the mysterious way the fog and mist shrouded the beach stirred up her memories.

That was the only time Mom-Mom ever really spoke of Frank, his alcoholism, the breakup of their marriage, and surviving with my mother during the Depression's challenging years. My nature is to be inquisitive and my training as a journalist and a spiritual director taught me the right questions to ask to get to the heart of a matter. But I never asked my mother or grandmother very much about those years and all that happened.

It always felt like something better left alone.

Throughout my childhood, my mother kept a small, yellowed, black-and-white photo of her smiling father holding her as an infant, right next to his cheek like a proud papa. She stored it in the top drawer of her dresser, along with her beautiful lace and linen handkerchiefs. One day, when I was about eleven years old, I opened the drawer and saw the picture ripped into pieces. I closed the drawer quickly.

At some point years later, my mother had the photo repaired and enlarged. Thereafter, she displayed it in a frame on top of her dresser alongside a wedding-day picture with my father until the end of her life. A few years before my mother died, I finally asked her how the picture got ripped up. She said she didn't know, perhaps Mom-Mom had done it.

The memory of that ripped up, yellowed photograph and the backstory of the difficult lives Frank, Mom-Mom, and my mother shared together always stayed with me as a reminder of the generational hurt and damage caused by untreated alcoholism. And it was one of the strong nudges that pushed me to seek help for myself when I was thirty-four-years-old *before a lot of awful stuff happened.* I did not want my legacy to my own children to ultimately become that painful secret stuffed away in hurt hearts.

Alcoholism is both a physical disease and a disease of the attitudes. In 1990 I was on vacation in Rhode Island, complaining to my mother about everything in my life. The truth was, I had so much to be grateful for. But I was full of that old demon RID. I also told my mother I had a growing desire to have a drink at night after my children were asleep.

My mother didn't mince words with me as we sat out on the deck on a beautiful July afternoon.

"Look in the mirror, Nancy. Look at yourself. You have a terrible attitude and you are blaming everyone else for it. Look at the woman in the mirror and *do* something about it."

I didn't like my mother's bluntness. I didn't like it one bit. But I knew she was speaking a truth to me about myself and she was doing it with love and a greater good in mind.

She encouraged me to try out a 12-step meeting.

"What do you have to lose? It's an hour of your time and a dollar in the basket."

What do you have to lose?

My mother returned home, and Joe and I continued our beach vacation with Annie, who had just turned four, and eighteen-month-old JP. We went to a barbeque at the home of good friends from our newspaper days. I had two beers that night, and I stood looking out at Ninigret Pond at sunset while the children played near the shoreline, hoping the same pattern of feeling sick and mightily pissed off the next morning after introducing alcohol into my system wouldn't happen.

But it did.

The next day at breakfast in a local restaurant, a meal that should have been a fun family time, I had a crashing headache and felt terribly nauseous. My body just could not tolerate and metabolize alcohol. My mood was a pretty dark that morning, too. And sitting in the restaurant with our kids and Joe on one of the few vacation days his schedule allowed, feeling so miserable, with my mother's words fresh in my mind, I decided I was done.

What do you have to lose?

I started to go to meetings.

I jumped in with both feet and took the suggestion to attend ninety meetings in ninety days to test the waters of applying the program's principles in my life. For the first few meetings, it was hard to connect the dots between my knowing deep in my bones that I had a growing dependence on alcohol and the war stories of those guys in the room. But I was told to *identify with the feelings—not compare stories.* And when I did, I knew my feelings of insecurity, anger, fear, ingratitude, blame, and anxiety lined up pretty damn well with what others described. Knowing my family's history and my mother's words of encouragement helped cut years of potential misery out of my future.

I began attending different meetings and found several I really liked. The meeting led by Brian and Gwen was my favorite of all. After listening to me "share' at a few meetings, Brian figured out I was a complete over-doer and *that* pattern of behavior—creating weekly commotion to keep up with all I had heaped on my plate—was a significant reason why I felt the need to have a glass of wine at night. Brian is one of the smartest men I know, and, like many very bright guys, he has a terrific sense of humor, which he skillfully used to disarm and teach at this meeting.

"So, Nancy, what do you have going this week? A neighborhood Halloween party for 120 kids? Running a retreat for 40 teenagers? Maybe we could all go to your house for dinner this Sunday—there would be only about 50 of us there!"

I would laugh along with the rest of the crowd at his deftly delivered insight, but more importantly, I began to get the memo that I didn't need the rush of approval from doing too much to validate my existence. As the weeks went on, Brian and I grew to be friends. We would talk after the meetings. We had a lot in common. We both were the oldest children of large Irish- Catholic families with alcoholism in our family histories. Like Joe, Brian ran his own demanding and successful business.

At this point, Joe was wondering about this whole meeting gig in my life. Joe didn't think I needed it because he did not think I had any dependence on alcohol. I knew he would like Brian and would have a better understanding of what it was all about by talking to him. We invited Brian over to our house for a Sunday dinner, and the two of them immediately hit it off. The friendship our families share, which grew after I introduced Brian to his wife, now spans more than twenty-six years.

Over these years, Brian and I have shared many conversations about the disease of alcoholism and its impact on families. When my children were younger, I told him how I deeply feared that they would fall into the trap. Brian answered me with great conviction:

"You've broken the chain. *You have broken the chain.* You came in and got help for yourself. You work at staying sober. You have broken the family chain of alcoholism. Your children will be OK."

Brian's words were a great comfort to me, and I have always trusted his judgment. I held on to what he said: by getting sober I would ensure that my own children would be safe. At the time, I took his words literally. As life happened with JP, I remembered that conversation with Brian.

How could things have gone so wrong?

My two older children were babies when I began going to meetings; my two younger daughters were not even born. I believed that by deciding to get help early on it, would serve as some kind of protective shield against my children being afflicted with this disease.

Clearly, I was wrong about any notion of a protective shield. It was as if I had watched too many Star Wars movies, because I know now that once my children became adults, there would be very little in life I could protect them from. But with the benefit of time, I have come to believe the decision I made more than twenty-six years ago to participate in a 12-step program, and the support I received from my husband and my mother to do so, did help break the chains of this disease for my family.

It just didn't happen the way I expected or wanted it to.

The generational impact of this disease in my family now spans more than ninety years. My grandmother was a young woman faced with the impossible challenge of trying to create a stable family life with an alcoholic spouse in the early 1930s. Hundreds of miles away, AA was just beginning in 1935 in Akron, Ohio, when Bill W., a Manhattan stockbroker, and Dr. Bob, a surgeon, met and shared their struggle.

Frank had few if any supportive resources to help him to battle his disease. My grandmother did not have the support she needed to help her deal with the fallout from his addiction. They both lived in the shadow of great misunderstanding and shame for their circumstances. Without the necessary help, Frank died of alcoholism. It took tremendous strength and courage for my grandmother to make the tough-love choice to prevent further escalating disruption in her life and the life of her baby daughter.

Four decades later, United States First Lady Betty Ford's public disclosure of her addiction to alcohol and opioids and the establishment of a treatment center in her name began to ease the societal stigma and misunderstanding surrounding the disease of addiction. The growth and acceptance of 12-step programs, education about the illness of addiction, and increase in treatment opportunities have vastly opened the way for greater help for addicts and their families. The current opioid epidemic in our country has brought further attention to the need for comprehensive, affordable treatment on every level. These many initiatives since the late 1970s have benefitted families like mine.

But, unfortunately *none* of this help, education, acceptance, or support was available to my grandparents and because of that, their lives, sadly, were ridden with shame and struggle, and ultimately a death sentence from addiction.

My grandmother set a powerful example of standing up for her family at great personal cost.

She broke the chain.

Chapter 12

HINDSIGHT IS 20/20

NANCY

It's hard for parents to get the tough-love thing. It is completely unnatural and counter-intuitive to what you believe you should do as a parent. It asks you to stop protecting, stop providing, and stop watching out for your child. It tells you to step back, walk away, and cut loose.

If addictive choices are the burning building your child is trapped in, tough love says: Do not run in and save your child from the flames. Watch them become engulfed in the blaze until they make the decision to run out of the building themselves—or not.

Who can do that?

Before Joe and I fully understood our role in the dysfunctional dance of family and addiction, we tried to do the tough love thing with some success, but we met with a lot of failure because we were inconsistently committed to letting JP live with the consequences of his choices.

As my mother told me: "You threw the mattress under him instead of letting him fall on the floor."

We tried. But for the circumstances we were in, well, it just wasn't *enough*.

How far back do you go trying to figure out what you did wrong? As I have sifted through the past, I know we could have spared our family a lot of pain if we had acted sooner than we did.

I still to this very minute carry guilt for choices we made for JP when he was young. Should he have attended a different elementary school? Were we wrong to force him to play Little

League baseball when he disliked it so much? Should we have been stricter with him? Did we get him enough help for his learning challenges? Was I too critical of him?

JP was adorable as a child. From the get-go he had these qualities I loved. He was really funny. He was always on the move. He loved summers. He had a way of disarming people with his charm and humor. I loved all his energy. He was kind to younger kids. I loved watching him cook and build extensive racetracks in his room with anything he could find for his collection of little cars. I loved his curiosity and his ability to figure people out.

He was my little man—*my Manzo*.

School had a chilling effect on all these great qualities. Getting him to do homework became a daily battle. JP and his sisters were enrolled in our parish elementary school, a great faith community, which offered a traditional learning style with very little help for struggling students. By the time JP reached eighth grade, he was struggling academically. He became depressed. He came and told us so.

"I'm depressed. I am not interested in things. I feel sad inside. I don't feel like doing anything."

We got help for him quickly. We found a well-recommended psychologist for JP to meet with once a week, and he eventually suggested a psychiatrist. In retrospect, this is where events started to veer off the road. JP started ninth grade at a Catholic high school and was drawn like a moth to flame to a rough, partying crowd.

The psychiatrist recommended a low dose of an antidepressant for JP. A few weeks later, she raised the dose. She told us to come back in ten days, but to call if I had any concerns.

JP's behavior began to change. It came on suddenly and strangely. There seemed to be no controls in place in his brain. He somehow got his hands on a BB gun, which he initially kept well hidden from us, and shot out the basement windows. He went into a friend's house and downed a can of beer. Then he came home and told us about it.

Late one evening, JP was incredibly restless. He spoke

about wanting to kill himself. I called the psychiatrist and described what was happening. She said we needed to immediately stop the medication and that JP would have to be watched closely because he was exhibiting a reaction known as disinhibition. She started to suggest that he be hospitalized while the medication levels dropped off. Panic gripped me.

What the hell is going on? This medicine was supposed to help, not make him feel worse. She wants him in a hospital? What is happening to my son?

Looking back, I was naïve about how dangerous this situation was for JP. I promised the doctor I would watch him closely and keep him home from school for several days. Ironically, at this same time, the media began publicizing government hearings on the effect of these medications on the undeveloped adolescent brain. I heard the testimony of parents whose children committed suicide while on these prescribed drugs, which completely messed up their brain chemistry.

JP

I remember being very depressed. I was spending most of my time in the basement of the house. I didn't want to do anything. I was very sad.

I don't know what brought this on. But if you read about depression, I was a textbook example of the symptoms.

I felt like I was in a bottomless pit, and mentally I was plummeting lower and lower every day. I remember crying for no reason. My parents took me to a counselor and then to a psychiatrist, who put me on an antidepressant.

After a few days, I remember feeling kind of better, albeit still spending most of my time in the basement.

I remember lying on the couch in the basement. I had a runny nose and I wanted to spit. And instead of going to the garbage can, I remember just spitting on the wall.

It seemed logical at the time. It was an impulsive thing.

What was happening was that I had lost my impulse control because of the medication. That wall was now plastered in my spit, which I know was disgusting, but I want you to understand how far off base that medicine had taken me.

Earlier that day, I went grocery shopping with my mom. I bought a box of 150 Slim Jims. While sitting in the basement, I ate all 150 Slim Jim's in an hour. Later that night, I went into the laundry room where my parents kept alcohol. There on the shelf were bottles of Cognac and Jameson.

Everyone was already upstairs in bed. I drank half of the bottle of Cognac and started walking back to the couch. About four steps in, I thought to myself, "I'm not drunk yet."

I turned around and drank a quarter of the Jameson. By the time I sat down, everything was spinning. I probably had alcohol poisoning.

I woke up the next morning with my face in a pile of vomit. When my mom saw that I was sick, I told her it was a stomach virus and not to worry.

Later that week, I snuck a BB gun outside with me. I shot out a couple of windows in the house, a computer screen in the basement, and the car windshield. I stole things blatantly.

I went in my parents' room and threatened suicide to get my way over some miniscule thing, which shows how distorted my thinking was at the time.

They knew there was a serious problem.

NANCY

JP's bad reaction to the antidepressant was the start of what became a series of unsuccessful attempts to find a medication to target his depression without harmful side effects. After the first debacle, the doctor prescribed another medication for JP, which seemed to work for a while. JP was already behind in his schoolwork from those months and he continued to struggle with it, but the depression itself eased. JP seemed to be back on his game.

The administrators at the Catholic high school JP attended were supportive. They saw the good in him and wanted him to succeed. At the end of his freshman year, we met with the school chaplain and the principal. It was decided that JP would be allowed to continue his studies there, provided he make up a religion and math class in summer school. He was also offered a summer job working at a Catholic seminary. It kept us busy because JP had to be in three different places at three different times in three different towns several miles apart every day.

That summer Grace was facing a serious medical challenge: she was losing her vision in her left eye. When we had brought Grace home from China two years before, we immediately began therapy for her badly crossed eyes with a pediatric eye specialist. But now the condition had worsened and we sought out another specialist. For many months, she had frequent doctor's appointments in New York City for her eyes, as well as speech therapy three times a week because, outside of our immediate family, no one could understand her when she spoke.

Joe's brother, Bob, was in from Hawaii and staying with us for several weeks that summer, and he offered to drive JP to all his commitments. He knew the time alone in the car with JP would also give him a chance to talk to his godson and encourage him to work hard and stay on track. We all deeply appreciated Bob's presence. He was always willing to pitch in to help with whatever needed to be done. Annie affectionately called him "Tim, the House Boy"— a nickname we all still use for Uncle Bob.

JP was getting up on time, enjoying his job working at the check-in desk at the seminary gymnasium, and keeping on top of all his school assignments. Joe, Bob, and I could see he was making headway. Before Bob left to return to Hawaii, he told us both he believed JP had turned a corner. We agreed.

We were all dead wrong.

Several times throughout the summer, JP went out with kids he met at summer school. Initially, there were no red flags on this one. He would meet the friends, grab a bite to eat or hang out with them in the neighboring town where they lived, and keep his 11 p.m. curfew. We met the friends one night when they came by the house to pick him up. They looked like nice enough guys, and we figured either way they were summer friends, who would disperse once school resumed in the fall.

We all headed up to our beach house that August for a family vacation. It was a time for the six of us to do all the things we loved to do together in the summer. What we didn't know then, probably mercifully, is that it would be the last Rhode Island vacation we would share with JP for a long time.

JP's sophomore year began uneventfully. But by November it was clear he was falling behind again. We restricted his going out. He was given mandatory study halls at school. This was not the only problem facing us. My mother was a patient in a Manhattan hospital, suffering the beginnings of paralysis from an unknown neurological disease. I felt hemmed in by problems: Grace's deteriorating vision, JP's poor behavior and school performance, and my mother's illness.

I knew enough to dig in deeper with the *God of My Understanding When I Didn't Understand*. I prayed a lot. I asked God to change these situations, and when they did not change but instead got worse, I asked God to give me the energy to meet the responsibilities I had.

There was a moment I can pinpoint on the timeline when I knew JP's situation was more than some simple adolescent dustup. It was the night of his high school Christmas concert. JP had really enjoyed being a member of the chorus in ninth grade. Joe and I were looking forward to going.

But two days before, JP announced another plan.

"You guys don't have to go to the concert on Friday. I've got a party to go to that night, and I am not going."

Not going?

On the afternoon of the concert, he answered the phone only once.

"I told you I'm not going."

"JP, Daddy and I will be at that concert. If you are not there, you will be grounded, and we will call the school."

At 7:30 p.m., we were sitting in the auditorium. The curtain rose, the chorus began to sing, and JP was nowhere in sight.

How could he blow this off?

He was defiant when he arrived home after curfew.

"You're going to rat me out to the school? Great parents you are!"

We took the phone away and grounded him until after Christmas.

It was clear the boundaries of some new dangerous game were being drawn. We needed to be ready for this.

Christmas pulled us all into a deeper family crisis: my mother was now paralyzed from the neck down. The uncertainty surrounding her condition was all consuming. Our children went frequently to visit their grandmother, whom they called Goggy, and pitched in at home while I spent several hours just about every day at the hospital. I hoped the seriousness of her illness would make JP realize he needed to be his best possible self.

The challenges that winter became a trifecta in late January when the second specialist treating Grace said she was going to completely lose vision in her left eye. The doctor was very gentle in delivering her assessment. At first, I couldn't even absorb it. By the time I got home, Joe was there. He reached out to a business contact at New York Eye and Ear Institute, who arranged for Grace to be seen two days later by Dr. Brian, a kind and brilliant pediatric eye specialist.

At some point during those weeks, JP's psychiatrist prescribed another medication, which did not work. Ultimately, after over a year with this doctor (who did not accept our insurance) and round after round of prescribed medications, none effective, we parted ways.

Looking back, we had locked ourselves into a kind of tunnel vision with this doctor and the parade of others who followed because each had a diagnosis, each had a medicine, each initially gave us hope that *something* could be found to help our son. But after several months of office visits, consultations, evaluations, and the obvious—lots of checks written for services not covered by our insurance plan—we would come up empty handed. Then it was on to the next doctor *as the one with the answers* recommended by someone whose opinion we valued.

With the benefit of 20/20 hindsight, these doctors all had code numbers from the diagnosis book for JP's behavior, but neither Joe nor I ever heard much about substance abuse from them. Maybe it was because they were relying on JP's account of his activities, which greatly minimized his substance use. But it was not until very deep into the events of JP's life that the dots were connected, tying his behavior to addiction.

Doubts about all these doctors were starting to creep into my mind. I asked myself, if a doctor's "specialty" is a particular diagnosis—if that's what the specialist has written books about and gone on TV talk shows to discuss—wouldn't he or she be more likely to *read that diagnosis* into JP's actions? Increasingly, I wasn't buying it. And I was getting angry with myself for getting jerked around by JP's behavior.

There was so much going on I felt like an ambulance chaser. I never knew the true meaning of the word *exhausted* till that winter. I wish I could say I had some great spiritual revelations at that point to help me through. But I didn't. I prayed the Rosary a lot because its repetitive nature was about the best I could muster—and it was comforting. I sought spiritual refreshment when I could—at daily Mass, at meetings, and with my spiritual director. I shouted out to God, "Please help us."

The answer to those prayers came in the form of being able to *show up time after time*. God gave us all the strength to show up with encouragement for my mother, now diagnosed with an autoimmune disease that left her in constant pain, paralyzed, and confined for months to a hospital bed overlooking the Hudson River. We did our best to help Grace negotiate a world with worsened vision and extreme sensitivity to light as Dr. Brian began the long-term treatment of chemical patching to restore vision in her left eye. It was hard for all of us to watch Grace squint in bright light and hold things inches away from her left eye to see. We also were following all the speech therapist's recommendations to help her.

Grace's name means "gift from God," which Annie, Molly,

and JP chose at a family dinner, ten days before we left for China. That name has always been a perfect fit. Having a very active toddler in a house of tweens and teens was a great, joyful adventure. Grace loved to sit inside the big guinea pig cage to play with those squirmy creatures and then drive them around the house in a little basket in her scooter. She scooped her Beta fish out of its bowl with her hands, placed it in a tiny container, and hid it under her bed blankets. (I found the poor fish a day later under soaking wet sheets— it went on to live three more years.) She took rolls and rolls of gift wrap, newspaper, and tape, wrapped up anything else she could find, and then presented these to us as gifts.

Grace, more than anyone, was JP's mainstay in the family. When he walked in a room, she would immediately jump into his arms and knock off his baseball hat. He would carry her around the house. They watched cartoons and made snacks together. They surfed the staircase in a laundry basket, and JP rode her around the backyard in her red wagon tied to his electric scooter.

Those were very happy moments, interspersed with JP's increasingly oppositional behavior. And it was about to go further south at a high rate of speed.

Chapter 13

BAD 2 WORSE

NANCY

JP was staying out past curfew, failing to get up for school, and getting verbally abusive. There were daily battles between us, which usually ended in both of us shouting.

Every morning, JP's alarm would go off and he would sleep right through it. I would go in and try to rouse him—always unsuccessfully. The school bus would come, blow the horn, wait for him, and then pull away. My anxiety would begin to skyrocket. I would get the girls off to school and come back home to find JP still sleeping in bed.

How can he just lie there? How can he let himself miss school? What is wrong with him?

I would then launch into a wake-up campaign: going into his room and turning on the lights, turning up the radio, pulling up shades, opening windows, pulling off his blankets, and, sometimes, even trying to flip the mattress over to get JP from horizontal to vertical.

My efforts would be met with a string of language from our son.

Eventually, he would get up and take the train to school, where there would be detentions waiting for missing classes.

The pattern went on for days that stretched to weeks. His behavior was putting a strain on our family and driving a wedge between Joe and me. Our approaches to managing our son were very different. We would argue over how to discipline him. We were losing any semblance of control we thought we had.

One of the worst nights took place on a Saturday in February. I had come home from a long day at the hospital with my mother, who needed to wear diapers and could no longer care for or feed herself.

Later in the evening JP came in. We got into an argument over his broken curfew the night before. I told him he had to stay in. Things had deteriorated so much I would stay up to essentially keep guard over JP to make sure he did not leave the house. But that night I was worn. I told Joe I needed to go to bed and left him in charge of JP.

Once I was up in bed, JP saw the chance to make his move. He began arguing with Joe and announced he was leaving for the night. Joe was not in the mood to put up a fight.

"Do what you want, JP. I am sick of this with you."

JP took Joe at his word. He called a cab. I was sleeping lightly and heard the cab door slam outside our home. I went down to see what was going on. Joe was sitting in the living room reading the newspaper.

"Where's JP?"

"He left."

I began to loudly blame Joe for walking away from his parental responsibilities. Joe argued back equally loudly that he wasn't a guard. We were angry and deeply frustrated with each other and the situation.

JP came home very late that night. The next day when he got up we saw that he had a black eye and the side of his face was swollen with bruises.

What the hell happened?

"A fight with some kids. They jumped me."

I went ballistic.

"What are you doing!? Who are these kids? How did this happen? What are you getting mixed up in? Don't you see you are destroying your life?"

Then I went after Joe.

"You can't sit idly by and read a newspaper while your son calls a cab to take him to who the hell knows where and gets beaten up. What are you thinking? I can't do this myself twenty-four hours a day."

My tirade yielded the same response from both: dead

silence. JP was in a free fall, and Joe and I were pretty much on different planets as to how to address it. Joe's course of action was to pull back and let JP's poor decision-making reap its own consequences. Mine was to enlist every counselor, doctor, and professional and attempt—pretty unsuccessfully—to put some consequences in place.

With a chasm between us, JP could just barrel through the middle. We asked to meet with the psychologist who had been treating JP for about eighteen months. We had hoped his patient, laid-back approach would give our son the space and support he needed to sort through his life. Clearly this wasn't working. The night of our appointment, the psychologist said so himself and expressed concern about the level of violence involved in JP's group of friends. His advice was to take our efforts to supervise JP to another level.

And what would that be?

He recommended we see an educational consultant and look at alternative boarding schools. My head felt like it was being twisted off and spun around like a top. More wizards, more money, more time chasing the wind. While he asked us not to hold him to a number, the price tag on an initial consultation was several hundred dollars. He mentioned a boarding school with campuses in Maine and Connecticut, which had helped another one of his clients. The cost was equivalent to a private college tuition.

"So, you are recommending this school for JP?"

"I am not expert enough about the schools to make a definite recommendation, and that's why you need to see the educational consultant."

"You've been seeing my son every week, sometimes twice a week, for over a year and you can't make a recommendation?"

"No, that's not my area of expertise."

OK.

We met with a consultant and learned there was a big world of wilderness experiences and boarding schools for "troubled teens." At the end of the hour, she said we would need to have a few more sessions to find the right placement and handed us a brochure listing her fees. On the drive home,

Joe and I began to talk in earnest *with each other* about what we could do.

We needed to work together. There were just too many leaks springing in the dam. We made the decision that we did not have a spare couple of thousand dollars to spend on a consultant, so we researched possibilities ourselves. This was when we began to use the word *racket*. We saw there was a whole lucrative business out there with a target market of desperate parents willing to do anything to help their children. Many were run by reputable professionals, but we learned others were not. Some of the programs were extreme. There was a school in upstate New York promising parents their kids would be on twenty-four-hour lockdown.

Were these off-track teenagers or career criminals?

We looked up the school mentioned by both the psychologist and consultant and liked what we saw: character education, academics, community, and tools for a productive life. In the midst of a mess spreading like an oil spill on open water, we felt we were onto something that might contain the damage.

I didn't want to send my son to a boarding school. All I wanted was for him to change back to the happy, humorous guy he once was, get to school on time, pass some classes, and be respectful at home.

Yeah, that wasn't happening.

Life brings people in your path when you most need them. I believe that's *Prayer Answering 101*: the saying "when the student is ready, the teacher appears," carries truth. But sometimes in the scramble for a solution, it is hard know the teacher has appeared. St. Teresa of Calcutta always spoke of recognizing Jesus "in his distressing disguise" as one of the poorest of the poor. A lot of solutions are initially veiled in a "distressing disguise."

So, we were really surprised at how we connected with this school at an informational meeting, which JP refused to attend. We heard young men and women, just like our son, tell the stories of how they were entrenched in negative choices and how the school's support helped them to turn their lives around. We met Chris, the admissions director, who would later serve as a mentor to JP and an incredible source of support and encouragement for our entire family. We made an appointment for an interview at the school's Connecticut campus.

There was a little bump-up of progress for JP at his high school when they allowed him to go to Disney World for a chorus trip, even though his grades did not meet the criteria. The school president, a priest who was JP's history teacher, hoped the trip would provide him with a sense of community and help reestablish his footing. We appreciated the kindness every teacher and administrator showed JP there. But within days of returning, he lost momentum.

JP

All I wanted to do was party. I wasn't into hard drugs yet. What I did was drink alcohol daily and smoke pot daily.

My family lived in one of the most affluent suburbs in the country. But I didn't want to follow their footsteps. The person I aspired to be was someone who lived in a low-end neighborhood with easy access to alcohol and marijuana and no expectations to do much with his life.

I didn't want to work. All I wanted to do was drink and smoke pot. That was the only time I felt happy. I didn't understand why this was such a problem to the police officers who told me I couldn't drink in public, and to my parents and administrators at school.

I was kind of waiting for everyone to say: "OK, you can drink and do whatever you want. We will leave you alone."

But that didn't happen.

NANCY

The reality of how bad things were became clear one night when JP left the house after we grounded him for missing a curfew. He showed up with friends a few hours later. We told him that his friends needed to leave, and he needed to come in.

He stood outside our house and loudly let loose with cursing and then spit several times at the family room window. I was horrified at the degrading act and, honestly, I was angry. We locked all the doors and windows. He slept in the car in our driveway that night.

The interview at the Connecticut boarding school couldn't come fast enough.

Chapter 14

MAINE

NANCY

We arrived at the boarding school with JP, not knowing what to expect. The three hours we spent at the interview with Chris offered more insight than all the counseling we'd had for the last three years.

Chris pointed to a photograph of himself sitting on a mountain when he was a student at the school's wilderness program. The photo captured a turning point in his life because it was while there that he decided to change life to a more positive one. After JP turned down his offer to come to the school, he asked JP to wait in the hall. Chris then turned his laser focus on us. There was no doublespeak.

"You need to take some action here," he said, "because what you are doing is not working and it's only going to get worse."

Joe and I were convinced that the school was a good fit, and we enrolled JP in the summer program, which would begin in mid-July. Chris also told us about the school's wilderness program in Maine, in case we needed a placement for JP before the Connecticut summer school started. During the ride home, we tried to talk to our son. But he fell asleep in the car.

With three months left until the school summer program, we needed more supports in place while JP still lived at home. So, we decided to use the PINS Program (Persons In Need of Supervision) offered by the county, which helps struggling young adults through weekly meetings with a parole officer supervising school attendance and behavior at home and in the community. They recommended JP enroll in an outpatient program for young adults dealing with substance abuse. Up to that point, no one had definitively decided JP had an addiction problem, but the hemorrhage from lack of school attendance and disruptive behavior were clear indicators *something* wasn't going right.

Throughout these weeks, there were brief moments when JP connected with the professionals who were trying to provide guidance. There were lots of phone calls and appointments with school officials, teachers, psychiatrists, psychologists, medical doctors, tutors, PINS people, priests, and addiction professionals. At the same time, our three daughters had their own lives and needs. Grace's vision therapy required appointments in Manhattan every ten days. After six months in the hospital, my mother was discharged to a residential physical rehabilitation hospital forty-five minutes north of our home, so she could learn to walk again.

In June, after meeting with the psychologist, we decided to have JP go to the wilderness program at end of the school year until the summer program began in mid-July. We still were not even sure how we were going to get him up to Maine—a twelve-hour car ride away. But over the next few days, with his anger and defiance growing, it was clear we needed to act more quickly.

It was time for JP to head north to the great state of Maine.

We knew of stories about young people being whisked off in the middle of the night, by paid muscle men, and delivered to wilderness programs. We did not want to go that route. Our hope was that the transition to Maine would be less dramatic. We came up with a plan: Joe would bring JP to our house in Rhode Island for Father's Day weekend under the guise of getting outside yard work done. I would stay home with our daughters until Sunday and pack up his gear. Then I would take a train to Rhode Island, and the three of us would hit the road to Maine.

The big unknown was how to accomplish this without having JP bolt once he learned where he was headed.

JP

My parents sent me to our summer house with my father after my latest run-in with the police, when I was caught drinking and charged with disorderly conduct. I had been taken to the police station where my parents had to come get me.

It was almost the end of the school year, and summer was so close I could taste it. In New York, the air changes and has a different scent nearing the summer months. I knew that once summer came, instead of drinking and going out only on weekends and some nights, I would be able to drink all day and all night.

There was a big three-day carnival going on at a local church that everyone went to. Unbeknownst to me, the police departments of several local towns had formed a joint task force to track those with criminal behavior involving drugs and alcohol. The group of people I hung out with was on their radar.

I came home from the first night of the carnival drunk and high. My parents told me I was on lockdown for the remainder of the weekend. I told them in some loud choice words that wasn't going to happen and that I would be going out.

I slept in the house that night, but the following day, I ran out before they could stop me. I never came home and went to the carnival both nights. I was so intoxicated I don't remember much. Eventually I came back home and acted as if nothing had happened. My parents told me that I was going to Rhode Island with my father for two days.

NANCY

It was a huge relief not to be worrying about JP's where-abouts. Later in the day I took out the wilderness program supply list. Ironically, it read like the list of equipment we had put together when JP went to Boy Scout camp years before. I was at K-Mart, alone, doing this shopping and talking to God.

Well, it was more like *questioning* God. Well . . . at least we were in a dialogue together.

"God, look at this. How did we get to this place? This list reads like a Scouting campout.

Why couldn't he just take that path? Maybe a few bumps in the road, some stupid boy stuff.

But this? *A wilderness program*? Where did Manzo go? Who is this gangster-wannabe in my son's body? What did we do so wrong here? Are we ever going to get this right??"

I felt a crushing sense of failure and responsibility for what had happened. The voice on the K-Mart loudspeaker should have announced: "Attention Shoppers: There's a total mess of a mother in the camping equipment aisle. Please send a cleanup crew," because I just stood there staring at the shelves, wondering how the hell we ever got to this point and fighting back tears in such a public place.

Our family was fractured. Some families navigate better than we did, some worse. Logically I knew that. But on a deeper level, shame and sadness ripped me apart. I felt I had failed, horribly, at raising our son.

We were a family that did things together. Supper together every night, family trips, vacations every summer at the beach, leaf-raking chores, church on Sunday, Giant football games, visits to grandparents, and family movie nights at home.

How did it go so wrong?

I wanted my Manzo back. I wanted the son back who went with me to Taco Bell and danced with me at family parties. I wanted the son back who loved cooking in the kitchen, skiing with his father, and tubing with his sisters in the summer. I wanted back the son we all laughed with.

And we were a long way off from that.

It was almost impossible on that Father's Day, while other families were gathering for barbeques, to see that we were doing something proactive to change the course of the downward spiral. Boarding the train to Rhode Island, I knew we had crossed over to another realm of parenting JP. We were enforcing the message that we would no longer tolerate his choices and behavior. Leaving the girls underscored the rupture in our family. Joe and I off chasing solutions for JP—

our daughters at home without us—on a day we all should have been together. That would be a blueprint for the way we operated for a while.

It was not a good one at all.

The train ride followed the beautiful Connecticut coastline. I pulled out my Rosary and began to pray to the Blessed Mother for this plan to go smoothly and for our family—all six of us—to come out the better for it. Surprisingly, a sense of peace settled over me.

The train pulled into the Westerly station where Joe and an unsuspecting JP were waiting. My heart began pounding, anticipating JP's explosive reaction. The minute JP saw me carrying the baggage, he knew something was up.

"Hey what's going on here? Where are we going? Why does Mom have all that stuff?"

Once Joe got on I-95 heading north, he told JP his behavior and choices were unacceptable for our family and we were taking him to a Maine wilderness program. JP began furiously kicking and pounding on the locked doors and windows. It was a good thing Joe was driving because the commotion in the back seat frightened me. For a moment or two, I thought JP was going to break the car windows. The lashing out, cursing, and threats continued for miles.

Then a calm came over JP, and for many hours he spoke about what he had done and how badly he felt about it. It was like a confessional right there in the car. He was candid about the extent of his substance use and the trouble he was in. He went into a lot of detail about how his life and behavior were unraveling.

He even went *way back* to when he would tease his sisters.

"Remember when Molly said I was making faces at her behind her back and I told you I wasn't, and you believed me? Well, I was."

Joe and I listened. We appreciated JP's honesty and, in a strange way, the opportunity the ride gave us to talk together. That hadn't happened for a long time. At one point, JP said we needed to stop the car, to use a bathroom. Joe was taking no chances.

He handed him an empty coffee cup.

JP

I got up to Rhode Island and did a couple of odd jobs with my dad. We spent the night there. When it was time to leave, we got in his car and the first odd occurrence happened. My dad asked me to sit in the back seat, which I did. He didn't get on the highway to head back to New York. I sensed there was something going on, and I asked him where we were headed.

"We are meeting your mother for dinner and then heading home," he said.

He pulled into the train station and began circling slowly. I could tell he was wasting time and trying to make conversation. I then saw my mother get off the train with a couple of large suitcases. Something was very fishy, but I hadn't figured it out yet.

We were now on the highway headed north. My anxiety and agitation went through the roof.

I said to them, "I know that you are fucking playing with me. Where are we going?"

"You are going to a wilderness program," my father said.

I felt like a piano fell on my head. That taste of summer and alcohol was slapped from my mouth, and the taste of blood, angst, and regret now filled the void. My very small world was beginning to crumble at a very rapid rate.

My dad was probably driving over 60 mph, and I remember contemplating jumping out the window because the child lock was in place on the door. I threatened to have my friends come get me when we stopped. I threatened to run away. That's how badly I wanted to continue drinking and partying. We drove for hours. When I calmed down, I started to come clean with my parents about what was going on in my life.

NANCY

It was after midnight when we stopped in New Hampshire. Joe and I pushed the bureaus and other furniture in the room in front of the door, so we would know if JP tried to leave.

We were in some little town in a rundown, roadside motel with our son. Our three daughters were far away at home. JP went to sleep immediately. For a long time, Joe and I lay awake in the dark in that cramped room that smelled like cigarette smoke, mold, and old food. We didn't talk. We didn't have to. Late that night, the silence was kind of soothing and there was comfort knowing we were there for each other and for our son.

The next morning, JP seemed resigned. We finished the drive to Maine pretty much in silence. We arrived at the school, filled out forms, and then it was time to say goodbye. In a complete misreading of the situation, I hoped an epiphany would take place: JP would tell us he loved us and understood why we brought him to Maine. The *Secret Belief* was peeking out from my heart.

That was to come much later.

I reached out to hug JP, but he pulled back, glared, and walked away.

We headed home. Joe needed to be in Manhattan early the next morning. Although we were exhausted, we were also relieved knowing JP was where he needed to be. We stopped at a frozen custard stand. Our outlook brightened as we sat at a picnic table in the sun, eating our cones. It was a gorgeous June afternoon, we had never been to Maine together before, and damn, that frozen custard tasted good.

We might as well make the best of this.

So, we drove to Freeport to visit the L.L. Bean flagship store. Joe and I shared a good laugh there, which we always remember, probably because laughing together after what the previous days had been was a pretty decent accomplishment.

Toward the end of our visit to the store, Joe, who can't pass up a bargain, gravitated to a large bin of returned canvas bags stitched with monograms and names. He stood there for a good ten minutes, picking up bag after bag to see if there was one we could bring back for someone whose name or monogram matched.

I stood across the room watching Joe. In the haze of punch-drunk exhaustion, given the fact that less than twenty-four hours before we were pushing furniture up against a door to contain JP, his bag-picking efforts seemed funny in an absurd sort of way.

"Hey Joe, what are you *doing*? You can just order a bag with a name on it."

He looked up from his labors and grinned. We both started laughing. I've always felt proud of the decision we made to carve out some "us" time. I think one reason we have a strong marriage is because over the decades, we have deeply valued resilience.

JP

We drove probably six hours north into the middle of nowhere in Maine. My parents left me there and were being nice and saying goodbye, and I was so mad at them I didn't even respond.

I then got on a school bus and was driven north for another four hours, and if I previously said I was in the *middle* of nowhere in Maine, I was wrong. That was a bustling city compared to the moose and pine needles I was now surrounded by deep in the woods. Not to mention five million annoying mosquitos and other flying creatures—and I hate bugs.

I got out of the school bus and saw four unshaven, unshowered grown men. I could smell their body odor from ten yards away, and I remember thinking to myself, "What the hell is going on here?"

One of them was wearing long johns as pants, and as I got closer, I started to hear what they were speaking about—these guys were actually arguing about who has the worst body odor. If you ask me, they all won—four blue ribbons. I introduced myself, making sure I let them know I had a horrible attitude.

I was then led on a trek for two miles to the tent that I was then told I would be calling home. Every inch of my body had a mosquito bite on it from that trek. I hadn't even made it to the tent and already I was ready to go home.

For the next month, I hiked all over mountains and heavily wooded mosquito areas. I ate vegetarian chili, which should be outlawed. It was a very uncomfortable and miserable time.

A very hot topic of discussion was—contingent on good behavior on the way back to civilization or "perceived" civilization—whether a stop at Burger King would be made. If you ever find yourself in a scenario where the best thing you can say is there is going to be a stop at Burger King, I would reevaluate where you are in life.

I was thinking I was going to be able to come home for the summer following completion of the wilderness program. In keeping with the theme of my life, I was wrong.

I did enjoy the Burger King hamburger though.

NANCY

JP sent us letters detailing the hardships with his own humorous spin on it. In one letter he wrote, "If I ever see you again, please bring me deodorant and a gun."

In another, where he wrote how much he missed us, it looked like the ink was running down the page from tearstains. Part of me was very touched by a display of sentiment and part of me was suspicious of a ploy. Much later on, JP admitted he made the tears with spit to gain our sympathy.

That was a prime example of the dynamic between us. I wanted badly to believe JP had experienced a change that brought back Manzo. For a long time, that desire always clouded my vision to the manipulation going on and the hard stance I really needed to take.

Chapter 15

DRAGGED

NANCY

We reunited with JP in mid-July to bring him gear for the summer program. The weeks in the wilderness seemed to agree with JP—though he didn't think so. JP was tan, healthy, and open hearted to us all. During lunch, he shared stories about his experiences hiking and working at a Maine light-house. He told us he wanted our family to visit it together and enjoy its natural beauty. He held Grace on his lap and joked with Annie and Molly.

JP spent the rest of the summer immersed in positive endeavors: sports, schoolwork, service projects, and a musical production. A month later we went back to participate in a family weekend, with two days of seminars aimed at helping families build on their strengths together. All of us had entered a supportive community of families, teachers, and other professionals.

JP

After completing the wilderness program, I spent the remainder of the summer in another behavioral education program in Connecticut until classes began at the boarding school. I was now in an environment where I was being challenged. The fact that I was still a teenager and very defiant, in addition to some of my alcoholic traits, made this a very difficult and trying time.

NANCY

JP's first semester went well. He played soccer, passed classes, and made friends, who were on track to achieve their own goals. Chris said JP was making progress but was struggling with the image he wanted to portray as a tough guy from the 'hood.

Overall, we were confident the school's expertise in dealing with young adults would "catch" him. But the second semester was a different story. JP found ways to undo the progress. He became friends with guys sneaking marijuana on campus. He feigned injury to get out of playing ice hockey. One night in January, he tried to run away. Chris followed JP and called us as he chased him down a dark road in the bitter cold. That night even Chris had reached his limit with JP. In January, JP was sent by the school to live in a yurt in freezing temperatures in Maine as an opportunity to reflect on his life.

JP

I basically spent the year pulling pranks, sneaking out, drinking, drugging, and getting into trouble. One night I wanted to drink very badly. I took a bottle of Listerine and sat in the bathroom stall and began drinking it. While I was in there drinking the Listerine, I heard one of the administrators calling my name in the hallway. I was already buzzed, and I was getting called to the Dean's Area for punishment for some rule I had broken.

The school would interrogate you and give you a piece of paper and tell you to get honest. I was sitting there with the dean and I burped, and he looked at me and said, "Why is your breath so minty?"

I looked at him and said, "Because I am drunk."

I then ran through the campus shouting that I was drunk.

I spent the next week on work crew.

NANCY

We supported the school's efforts to enforce a positive value system. But that spring brought more poor behavior by JP. He was denied the privilege of going home for spring break and went back up to Maine *again* to do the schoolwork he had missed for the previous weeks.

In late spring, school administrators scheduled a meeting with the three of us and said JP had not earned the privilege to be a senior. He needed to put forth extraordinary effort in the coming weeks to be promoted.

JP agreed to try to make that happen. His commitment was not that of a man with a fire in his belly for excellence, but he understood what he needed to do. For the next three weeks, reports came in that things were going well.

JP came home for Mother's Day weekend. One of the school's policies is that its rules are in place when a student is home on break and any infraction is dealt with by both the family and school. The first night we had a great time going out for pizza. In the morning, we all did a lot of chores together as we had just moved into an old, run-into-the-ground farmhouse needing tons of work. JP was happy to give us a hand with some of the heavier jobs. That night he said he wanted to go out with his friends for a short while. We set a 10 p.m. curfew. JP left at 7 p.m.

At 9:30, the phone rang and a man identifying himself as a sergeant at a nearby police department called the house looking for JP. I could not fathom how things could have fallen apart with JP in two hours and thirty minutes to the point that the police were looking for him.

In one of the biggest displays of cluelessness in my entire life, I asked the voice on the phone if the phone call was a prank.

"No ma'am, this is no prank. There was a disorderly conduct incident in town tonight. We were told it was your son. We want to speak to him."

The rest of the conversation was a blur. JP came home very late and clearly inebriated. We told him the police called looking for him. He made up a story. We told him we were not interested in some fictionalized account of his night and went to bed.

Joe and I decided JP should leave early instead of staying home to eat breakfast with the family and attend Grace's ballet recital. On the car ride to the bus, we told him we were disgusted with his behavior. I told him he ruined Mother's Day and more than likely ruined his chance to be promoted to twelfth grade.

None of this was well received by JP. His lack of remorse made me even angrier. My mood was a black one. And it threatened to spill over into the rest of Mothers' Day.

There was nothing I could do to change what happened the night before. I decided to focus on *the good, sweet, and lovely things* the day offered, and I asked God to please help me do so. I thought of Zen master Thich Nhat Hahn and his mindfulness practices. He says that when we do any simple activity we should see it as a " . . . a wondrous reality. I am completely myself, following my breath, conscious of my presence, and conscious of my thoughts and actions. There's no way I can be tossed around mindlessly like a bottle slapped here and there on the waves."[4]

Most of the time when things went south with JP, I was a bottle slapped around by the waves. But *that day* I practiced the discipline of focusing on the "wondrous reality" of Grace's ballerina glory as I applied bright red lipstick on her little bow lips, put her jumpy little feet—which are as wide as a box—into pink slippers, and gathered up her long, thick, black hair into a ballerina bun.

I was present for the gift of the present.

I wish I could say I was always able to shake off distraction, anger, and sadness. I lost a lot of time letting myself be pulled into the vortex of JP's choices caused by the disease of addiction.

---

4   Thich Nhat Hanh, *The Miracle of Mindfulness A Manual on Meditation* (Boston, MA: Beacon Press, 1975), 6.

It's what whalers long ago called a "Nantucket sleigh ride." When a whale was sighted by whaling vessels out at sea, crews set out in small, wooden boats armed with har-poons connected to the boats by lines. Once it was speared, the sailors let the whale take them on a "Nantucket sleigh ride"—dragging their vessel out in the open ocean until the whale exhausted itself and could be captured.

But sometimes the whale resisted surrender, dragging the boat and its unlucky crew far out to sea, where it would sink. I was on a Nantucket sleigh ride of my own and was a long way from figuring out how to cut the line.

Chapter 16

"YO HO, YO HO, A PIRATE'S LIFE FOR ME"

NANCY

After Mother's Day, the boarding school decided JP had to repeat junior year. It was a sound decision. But I knew it opened the door for an all-out war with JP when he came home for the summer. I also knew Joe had been counting on JP attending the school for only one more year because of the financial demands it placed on us.

The summer started out well enough. JP participated in two school-sponsored service programs, one on his own and one with Joe. But at the end of July, when he returned from the second trip, he launched a campaign to convince us he should not have to go back because he was doing *so much better* at home. He was helpful, respectful, and agreeable. Joe and JP began to have private conversations about attending the local high school. Our new (but old and in-need-of-repair) house was in one of the nation's top school districts. JP wanted to convince us its high school offered a new environment where he would succeed. I wasn't buying this because I knew the private school offered something the public school could not: a twenty-four-hour-a-day supportive community. But Joe, intent on the difficult bottom line of two more years of tuition and JP's clearly lackluster record there, was quickly moving toward jumping on the *Public High School or Bust Bandwagon*.

I felt outmaneuvered.

The boarding school had a saying: truth over harmony. Not sticking to that was how I made one of the biggest mistakes of my life. By summer's end, Joe's viewpoint won out. And I chose *harmony* with Joe and his choice over the *truth* I knew in my core: JP staying home and going to a new school was a bad decision.

JP

At the end of the school year, I knew that I had a small window and a slim chance to convince my parents not to send me back to boarding school. I was an altar boy for that entire summer. I drank a few times, but aside from that, I did not do any drugs or even get overly intoxicated.

At the end of the summer, by the grace of God, or perhaps Lucifer, my wish was granted. I went to enroll at the public high school as a senior.

NANCY

Joe called the school to tell them JP would not be returning. Teachers and administrators then called me. A conversation stands out from the school's headmistress.

"You need to stand up for your own truth, Nancy. You need to stand up for your family and do what you know is right. You *know* what is right."

Her words empowered me briefly. But my resolve to battle it out with Joe wilted. I didn't understand it fully then, but I know now it was the *cowardly route*. I did not challenge Joe and JP enough on the decision.

There was *backup* at the boarding school. There was around-the-clock supervision and support by teachers, administrators, parent groups, family seminars, mentors, and alumni. Joe and I were now alone, on our own, and the challenge of managing JP was bigger than both of us. JP began to blow off curfews, schoolwork, chores, family events, and respectful behavior.

A small fire was now doused with kerosene, and a blaze was about to ensue.

The public high school allows students a lot of freedom, and that kind of environment is a great fit if you are a motivated and disciplined student. But for JP it was the wrong fit, and the fact that he was arriving too late in the game to receive significant help created the ideal setting for him to become what can best be described as a *pirate*. JP looted and plundered every promise we believed he made in good faith. Too late I found my voice with Joe about the school switch. I had blinked and lost sight of the goal.

The pattern of not staying the tougher course kept replaying itself. That was where we went wrong. We wanted to believe his promises. We wanted to believe this time would be different from all the other times. And I wanted to be in harmony with Joe, not living in constant disagreement over how to manage our son. The other part of the problem was that none of us really understood the extent of JP's substance abuse. That understanding would come in time. But, unfortunately, we didn't see it clearly enough then.

The blowback from the school decision was JP's increased partying and increasingly threatening behavior to intimidate us into leaving him alone. Joe was adamant that the right decision had been made despite mounting evidence to the contrary. I think he just believed that until JP chose to get himself together, school would be a difficult road, so why spend more than $40,000 on difficulty? But I missed the support and structure the boarding school offered JP with academics, service projects, sports, and reflection groups.

The anger and frustration between all of us rose like floodwater in monsoon season. Having experienced a respite—even with JP's limited progress there—I keenly felt the difficulty of managing him at home. Within weeks, JP gained the notoriety of being the biggest badass at the new high school.

Now that's something to be proud of.

He made fast friends with students who spent their time

cutting class and hanging around the parking lot, smoking cigarettes. The school offered support services, and his academic dean was encouraging and available. The problem was that for JP, the new school was just another playground where he could run with scissors in his hands.

Our family was in a new home. It should have been a time of adventures for all of us. It was, in part. Grace adapted well to the nurturing environment of her elementary school. Molly made a lot of friends and played field hockey while juggling the academic demands of freshman year. Annie was enjoying life at college. But for me, all the good moments were largely overshadowed by the quicksand of JP's life.

Joe, JP, and I were locked in a stone-cold standoff. Every time something went wrong with JP, I would think about how it would be *different if he had followed through at the boarding school.*

I was living in the problem, not the solution. What made this time the most difficult was that Joe and I *weren't on the same page.* We were tossing blame back and forth like a game of Hot Potato played with a loaded grenade.

One school day, mid-morning, I heard some noise in the driveway and looked out a bedroom window. JP and a bunch of guys smoking cigarettes were standing around a car with heavily tinted windows in our driveway.

Why aren't they in class? What the hell are those kids doing hanging around my driveway?

I opened the second-story window, stuck my head out, and started yelling.

"JP, what are you doing here? Who are these kids smoking cigarettes on my property? Why aren't you in class? Is this what you want to do with your life—stand around some kid's car instead of going to class? You all leave here right now and get back to school!"

JP and the rest of the crew looked up. I don't think any of them expected to see me half hanging out a window, delivering a rant. With a quick nod of his head, JP motioned to his friends that it was time to go. They piled back in the car and drove off to find another (quieter) spot to fritter their time away.

These many years later, JP and I laugh about it. But that morning I was hopping mad and didn't give a damn that I let them all know it.

Late that autumn as things got worse, I called Chris to speak to him about my regrets. He shared the story of a family whose son did not want to return to the boarding school. The parents gave their son an ultimatum: return or we will throw you out of the house. The son chose the latter and was living a difficult existence away from home.

"The parents stood firm," Chris said. "You could do the same."

That story had staying power, but I couldn't imagine throwing my seventeen-year-old-son out on the street. I still believed that *somehow, somewhere* there was an easier solution. Deep down inside was the truth: I lacked the courage to even consider taking such a drastic step. But as the months wore on, the story kept surfacing in my mind and I knew it held an answer for our family.

JP

I had solidified my reputation as a deviant at my new high school within three months. I didn't really understand that you can't not work or go to school and just drink and do drugs all the time. But that's all I wanted to do. My selective vision would only show me that other people my age were doing the same thing.

The reason I say selective is because everyone else who was doing the drinking and drugging that I was doing was also going to school and working at the same time. The first few weeks of class went well. I knew a few people from my days of running around, and they knew me. I went to a party the second week of school where I drank and smoked pot.

Mind you, I hadn't smoked or drank that much in about four months. Once I did, I remember thinking: "How did I go so long without doing this?" And that I needed to start doing this every day again—which I did.

While my drinking, pot smoking, and pill popping picked up, my attendance at school dropped. At the time, I didn't see a relation between the two.

Within a two-month period, it was pretty much over for me at school.

Chapter 17

DROPOUT

NANCY

In January, the school launched what I can only describe as a campaign to get JP off its enrollment. I really couldn't blame them. JP had rejected any help the school offered. But when a member of the counseling staff started calling me *several times a day after every class* JP missed, it felt like harassment. Hour after hour, the phone would ring and ring and ring and on the other end was the counselor, telling me JP was not in a class and asking me what was I going to do about it.

I began to imagine this professional as a well-educated and well-compensated *bar bouncer* responsible for weeding out the undesirables who would tarnish the district's graduation stats. By the end of February, JP stopped going to school altogether and a tough shell of anger and frustration masked whatever was left of the son I once knew.

He had given up hope for himself and began to spend his days sleeping and his nights going out with his posse of pirates. A vampire existence. He developed a great way to keep us at a distance. Any effort to engage him in any kind of conversation was met with one-syllable answers. If we pushed beyond that, loud angry words and door slamming ensued.

JP's becoming a high school dropout was a low that I couldn't even comprehend. We had raised our children to value the gift of education. We live in an area where it is *considered the bare minimum* for children to graduate from high school. It is expected they will graduate from college and beyond.

I firmly believed I was a complete failure as a parent. I

questioned why God ever even *allowed* me to have the gift of four children and believed there was very little I had ever done right to raise them. Such dark thoughts swirled in my mind most of the time. I withdrew even further from the company of friends when I needed them most.

Insomnia set in hard. Every night I would wake up at 2 a.m. and stay awake for hours. Many nights, I reached over to my nightstand and grabbed my Rosary. Despair is pretty effective at blocking the sense of hope prayer can bring. But I repeated the Hail Mary, trying to recall the intense beauty and peace the Blessed Mother held for me when Joe and I renewed our commitment to our Catholic faith when Molly was baptized. The Blessed Mother's gentle maternal love had drawn me back to the Catholic Church then. I spent those sleepless hours trying to remember the beauty of Mary's presence when our family's life was filled with noisy fun and innocence. Other times, I would just lie in bed in the dark with sad thoughts playing a vicious game of ping-pong in my head.

There is a craziness in the addiction cycle of a family. It's a seesaw of emotions. I was angry at JP and heartbroken for him at the same time. The ammunition needed to disrupt this cycle is a hardnosed, unflinching plan for dealing head on with the addict and the illness. Up to that point, the professionals we sought advice from had missed the bull's-eye—and so had we.

The psychiatrist who was seeing JP had been recommended by the high school's "bouncer." This doctor did not definitively commit to saying JP had an addiction problem. When we spoke to him, it was sort of this "let him leave school, let him get a job, see if he can drink in moderation, and then we'll see what happens next." There was a terrible disconnect between what this guy was recommending and the reality of our son living vampire hours with increasing disruptiveness.

While JP was failing out, there were a few very simple things that illuminated my days.

And I mean very simple.

St. Teresa of Calcutta always urged others to "Do small things with great love." I put a lot of love and mindfulness into these small practices, and it helped me stay sane.

Really.

I volunteered to be a class mother for Grace, undoubtedly qualifying me as one of the oldest kindergarten class mothers in the annals of the school's history, as I was forty-six-and-a-half when we brought two-year-old Grace home from China. The teacher had a lively, creative classroom, including a pet lizard whose diet was live crickets. I agreed to be the mother responsible for purchasing the unsuspecting crickets twice a week from a local pet store and delivering them to the hungry lizard.

What the heck?

As *crazy* as it sounds, the routine of going cricket-shopping provided a kind of relief from the swirl of unpredictability engulfing me. Annie and Molly decided to surprise Grace by buying her a lizard of her own, so then I was buying two plastic bags of jumpy creatures each visit.

Chirp, chirp.

The other simple task was baking chocolate chip cookies for Molly's field hockey team a few times each week. I wasn't really someone who enjoyed baking. But strangely enough, this activity was soul satisfying. I loved the fragrance of the baking cookies filling the kitchen. I loved packing them up warm from the oven. I loved seeing the girls—dirty and tired after a game—dig in as they boarded the bus back home.

Wise St. Teresa knew small things done with great love give a gift to the giver, as well.

That fall I also began a new endeavor—co-teaching a twelfth-grade spirituality class at our parish. The irony was I would be teaching high school students at church while my own son was out on the town. But the opportunity to explore God's invitation with them was a source of comfort to me, and surprisingly, led to a new, deeply satisfying career working in youth ministry.

What's the take-home message here?

God uses the truly unexpected to bring us peace and to

help us along when we are struggling. I never would have imagined buying crickets, baking cookies, or faith sharing with high school students would help give order to my days and shore up my collapsing self-esteem. But when I prayed for help, *that* was how God saw fit to answer. Over time I realized those activities were odd, unsolicited points of grace, and I appreciated the consolation they provided even more.

As spring arrived, Joe and I agreed we had to pursue a more direct hit at the substance abuse issue. We were weary of chasing solutions, but we were *absolutely not going to give up on* JP.

It was at this time, that Dr. Cipriano became a part of our "team." He had a lot of wise sayings and stories that have stuck in my mind. One of the most powerful stories he told me was about a single mother he knew in his clinical work in a hospital. The mother had an addicted son. She threw him out of her apartment. The next day when she left to go to work, she opened her apartment door and found her son sleeping in the doorway.

And here's the "Aha!" moment: the mother *stepped over her son's sleeping body*, locked her apartment door, and went to work. When she returned from work she *stepped back over his sleeping body and locked the door for the night*. This mother repeated these actions every day for three weeks. Finally, after three weeks, the son knocked on the door and told his mother he would go to treatment. Dr. Cipriano recounted the story simply without embellishments. He knew the direction it was pointing me in, and he let its power speak to me.

It took me a long time to come to terms with what had to be done. Longer than it should have, really. Dr. Cipriano was blunt: JP needed to be out of the house. This fact frightened me at first. But as we spoke each week, I began to get more comfortable with taking a drastic measure.

Eight weeks after we began "the work" together, Dr. Cipriano suggested we get JP some kind of room outside of our home. In the three months since he failed out of school, he had been jobless and without direction. We were able to get him a room at the YMCA.

We stuck to that plan—for a while.

JP

My parents told me I was no longer welcome in the house because I was no longer in school. They informed me that my options were to get back in school in order to remain in the house or leave the house and move into the Y.

I, of course, saw an opportunity to be free. In my mind, the unfortunate circumstances I encountered in life were a result of my parents nagging me too much. They cared too much. It had nothing to do with my deviant actions.

I moved into the YMCA, and my drug usage and alcohol consumption were no longer monitored by my parents. My downward spiral gained a lot of momentum. My substance abuse and criminal behavior now kicked into high gear.

NANCY

JP became ill with pneumonia after living at the Y for a month. When he called and told me he was sick, I directed him to the family pediatrician. I wanted him to fend for himself. But then the pediatrician called me. He sounded worried. The doctor said JP was very ill and he needed to be home. I felt relieved to have an excuse to bring JP home.

I was sure that a month at the Y would be lesson. I was sure once he recuperated, he would be ready to finish high school and get on with his life. Not only was I sure, but JP told me this, *and* I believed him. So we let him move back home.

Initially, JP got a job and began to make plans to return to school in the fall. I went back to Dr. Cipriano, elated with the news. But he didn't share my outlook.

"Let's see if he keeps this resolve," he said quietly.

The job and JP's good intentions lasted through July. By August, he was not getting out of bed in the morning. Dr. Cipriano was not sympathetic to my frustrations.

"One month in the Y, then home on sick leave, then permanently home does not change someone," he said. "What would he do if you lived in another state? He'd have to go to an ER and then go back to his room and figure out how to take care of himself and get his life together. You have to do this longer than one month, Nancy."

I didn't like what Dr. Cipriano said. But there was no BS to it. There was truth to what he was saying. There was truth with compassion, not judgment.

I knew I needed to listen and then act on it.

In August, JP told me there was a program at the community college that would give him a GED by taking college-level courses and that he wanted to enroll in it. He seemed enthusiastic about this opportunity. He also attended a few 12-step meetings. I believed JP was being sincere. We went together to meet with an academic advisor and to pay the tuition. We went to the school store to buy textbooks, notebooks, and even a sweatshirt. I wanted to see something good happen. For those few first days when his classes started, it felt like *something* was happening. Maybe . . . *maybe this might be the answer*.

For more than a year, Joe had kept an old car parked in our driveway as a "carrot" for JP to pull his life together. He even took it to a mechanic to have it fixed up for JP. But the car just sat unused, month after month, as our son's behavior didn't warrant the reward of his father's old car. Joe would go out weekly and run the car for a while to keep the motor in working order.

Every so often, JP would sit in the car at night and listen to loud music. One day Joe came into the house and told me how it made him really sad to see the car parked there, as he had originally thought it would be an incentive for JP. Joe had tears in his eyes as he quietly spoke about how confounded he was by JP's choices and the car he so very much wanted to give his son remaining unused in the driveway. Joe rarely gets emotional, and seeing him that way was painful.

When JP enrolled in community college, with a lot of promises about getting his GED and about turning his life around, we decided to let him use the car to commute to school.

We believed he wanted to succeed at school as much as we wanted him to succeed.

But very late one Saturday night, he was driving alone and crashed the car at a deserted intersection. The car was totaled. Luckily, he was not hurt.

Within weeks, JP dropped out of community college. The disease of addiction is unrelenting.

JP

I started at community college not wanting to go to class, but to buy myself into the good graces of my parents and to get them off my back. At this point in time, I had tried a number of prescription medications and hard drugs, but alcohol and pot were my thing. I had never fully committed to anything heavier, although I had tried it.

I made acquaintance with an individual who sold cocaine while at community college. I then began doing cocaine on a nightly basis. I also began taking Xanax. The combination of the extremely powerful stimulant, cocaine, and the powerful sedative of Xanax put me in a manic state.

I *really* started to get crazy.

Some of the money I received to fund this habit came from stealing from my parents and from others. I quickly went from attending classes at community college to not attending any classes at all.

I really enjoyed the feeling cocaine gave me. I often relate it to feeling like Superman. It was a very strong experience. On the down side, my anger skyrocketed, my health deteriorated, and when I was not on a substance, my self-esteem—or lack thereof—continued to seesaw.

The hole that I was digging for myself with the shovel had now been replaced with a backhoe—and the pit was deep. I remember when I was coming down off the coke and I would take a handful of pills to speed up the process. This was a toxic combination. Mixing any stimulant and sedative can easily kill you.

Almost every night I would do this, and I would say to a friend, "My heart is beating funny, and if I stop breathing tell them this is what I am on."

I would often joke that I was on a toxic cocktail. I found this humorous at the time.

Chapter 18

THE GIFT OF DESPERATION (A.K.A. GOD)

NANCY

JP was in a free fall.

I could hear in my head Dr. Cipriano's story of the mother stepping over her sleeping son's body. But I still couldn't bring myself to do that. So, we continued on the path that had proven to be *completely ineffective,* but a lot *easier* to follow—lining up another psychiatrist for JP to see.

It was now December—more than ten months since JP failed out of high school. A friend recommended we take him to see a doctor specializing in Attention Deficit Disorder. At the risk of sounding completely stupid and clueless, the idea that the root of JP's problem might be ADD had a lot more appeal than the idea that he was an addict. We brought JP to a well-appointed Manhattan office to see the doctor's associate, as the other doctor's schedule was booked. He prescribed clonazepam for JP's anxiety in the hopes that by reducing his anxiety, he would be better able to attend and function at school.

OK. Sounds like a plan.

There wasn't a lot of discussion about substance abuse or his violent outbursts. Just a follow- up appointment in a few weeks. Leaving the city with Joe and JP that afternoon just before Christmas, I fell into the trap of believing we were on to the right solution *again*. That was always part of the hell of all these doctors. We always believed the next one had *the insight, the program, or the solution.*

Life offers light-filled gifts and dark gifts. No one ever misses the light-filled gifts—a child's hand-painted flower pot for Mother's Day, a friend's box of homemade brownies, or your daughter treating you to a manicure with her own hard-earned money. These are the soul's food.

But the dark gifts life presents are harder to recognize and even harder to embrace. How can the *Gift of Desperation* ultimately lead to freedom? Twelve-step fellowships talk about that gift, and it is no coincidence its acronym is *GOD*.

JP's life with access to prescribed clonazepam was a disaster in the making. His erratic, violent behavior rocketed. About two weeks after the doctor's appointment, JP came into our bedroom in the middle of the night and began shaking me awake. He leaned over the bed, practically pressing his face on mine. Even in the dim light, I could see he had a wild look in his eyes.

"Where are the pills? Where are those pills? I need one of those pills," he demanded.

"JP, it's 2:30 am. Just go to bed and go to sleep."

He raised his voice, insisting on me getting out of bed and giving him a pill.

His behavior was so abrupt and loud, and the look on his face so angry, I began to feel scared. Joe heard the commotion and told JP to go to bed. JP cursed and left the room. I couldn't go back to sleep. I stared into the dark and asked God for strength to do what needed to be done.

What we could not foresee was that the desperation JP was living then, and we along with him, was laying the groundwork for *the gift* to be born. I was not even able to see the connection between the prescription drug, which was supposed to help relieve his anxiety, and his behavior wildly spun out of control with it in his system along with other substances I didn't know about. That night I could not even imagine that the *Gift of Desperation* would lead JP to something wonderful—even miraculous.

At that moment, it just felt like the quicksand sucking us down.

I also learned JP was stealing from us. Initially I had some distant sense a few things were disappearing. A twenty-dollar bill gone from my wallet. A jar full of spare change suddenly empty. Now it was blatant. I realized some of my gold jewelry was missing. I had purchased a bunch of gift cards—they were nowhere to be found. Because of my own anxiety, I was operating in some kind of chronic brain freeze and thought I had misplaced the cards, jewelry, and cash.

But within a few weeks, I realized JP had taken it all.

He denied it, of course. But I knew that was a lie. It was another piece of evidence pointing to what we needed to do.

Dr. Cipriano began to explain the process of getting a court order of protection, *if we needed it, more like when we needed it,* to ensure that JP would not return once we told him to leave. There was this growing sense of dread about what was going to have to take place. I couldn't see then that forcing JP out would be the best possible thing for all of us. But fortunately, along with Dr. Cipriano, we had friends and family members who reinforced the message.

Months before, Big Jim, a longtime family friend and former Marine, had decided it was time to speak up, and he chose the morning of Joe's fiftieth birthday party to do so. Things were disorganized that morning as we prepared for the celebration, which included Jim and forty other guests. That week, JP entered a local outpatient addiction treatment program. The anger he harbored was right in our faces. I wanted to cancel the party. But Joe insisted we stay on track with our plans.

Big Jim pulled his white Cadillac into our driveway, gave the door one strong knock, and walked in. He knew he would see us later at the party, but he had something to say to Joe and me privately and he was never one to hold back. He had known me since I was eight years old and saw our family as his own.

"There are five of you, and one of him. There are five members of this family who deserve a happy life," he said slapping his hand on the granite countertop. "There are five of you and one of him. And it's time you do something. If you have to put him out, that's fine. He doesn't deserve to be here right now with the rest of you. I'll see you all at the party tonight. We'll have a great time."

He kissed me on the cheek and strode out.

There are five of you and one of him.

Months had passed and now it was just before Christmas. Big Jim's words, as well as all the others over the months, had tumbled around my mind like rocks in a rock polisher. It was time for action. So, in my mind, I set a deadline. It was my own deal with the devil. We would work to have JP leave our home in January. I did not want to ruin Christmas for our family. I actually believed we could somehow hold with all the traditions we enjoyed: decorating the kitchen with nutcracker soldiers, making gingerbread houses, caroling in the neighborhood, putting up the tree, and exchanging Kris Kringle gifts.

Fa la la la la.

This was lunatic thinking on my part—that a bunch of Christmas traditions would hold us all together while JP's addiction and acting out grew stronger every day.

And a partridge in a pear tree.

One of my siblings saw the strain this was taking on our family and asked my mother, "What are they doing? When is Nancy going to do *something*?"

"She is getting her strength for this," my mother replied. "She is getting ready to take action. But she needs to get strong enough to do it."

Each day I could feel my resolve slowly build—unfortunately *way too slowly* for the level of unraveling taking place, but building nevertheless. Joe and I were preparing ourselves for the inevitable: throwing JP out and then seeking a court order of protection to keep him out until he was ready to seek help.

We had dinner with JP and my mom for his birthday. We reminisced with family stories that made us all laugh. JP told us all he was going to make good changes in the coming year. We wanted to believe him. He thanked us, hugged us all, and left to go out with his friends.

At some point the next day he came home, crashed, and

woke up hours later like a crazed person. He tore his bedroom apart looking for something and in a rage, pounded his bare fist into the wall. The force of impact left a hole in the solid plaster. His hand was shattered.

What happened?

He left the house with a broken hand, coming back the next day to sleep. On Christmas Eve, when we were supposed to be taking Grace to be an angel in the pageant Mass, Joe was driving JP to the local emergency room for his hand. At my request, the rest of us skipped the pageant Mass in favor of a later one. I just couldn't handle seeing a lot of people I knew. At Mass I heard the beautiful words of the Gospel. The church was packed with families singing hymns. I felt like a fraud even being in church with my family in such tatters.

On Christmas morning, our daughters got up early to open gifts. Joe took movies of them running down the stairs as we had done since Annie was a toddler. We didn't attempt to try to get JP out of bed. Later we went to join my extended family for dinner. I don't think anyone knew how much pain we were in. No one asked where JP was. At some point, a relative made a sarcastic remark about my family and it was my breaking point. I stormed out. My family followed.

Merry Christmas.

During the car ride home, our daughters encouraged us to enjoy our own family Christmas. They suggested we head to Manhattan to see the Rockefeller Center tree and get some dinner. We stopped at the house to change into warmer clothes and found JP in the living room looking at the tree. He was calm and friendly.

"Hey, where have you all been all day?" he asked.

Molly filled him in. JP's hand was really swollen, but his mood was as if nothing had happened at all.

"Hold on. I'll get dressed and come to the city with all of you," he told us.

None of us expected to see JP sitting in the living room so relaxed and friendly. When he left the room to change his clothes none of us said anything. The five of us looked at each other and in some way wordlessly agreed *to just go with it*. We headed to the city and had hamburgers at a hotel near Rockefeller Center. It was a great time with a lot of laughter and family stories. We took pictures in front of the tree. It was an evening to be treasured. I still have those pictures on my phone.

It would be the last Christmas we would have with JP for a few years.

Once the holidays were over, Joe and I moved ahead with a plan of action. Dr. Cipriano stepped up the pressure of his recommendation for a court order of protection. Joe and I began researching treatment centers. We made a lot of phone calls and visited several places. We began to learn a lot about insurance coverage for inpatient detox followed by twenty-eight-day inpatient rehab.

JP's behavior became more erratic as the disease of addiction took over more and more. In the middle of one night, we woke up to the odor of paint in our bedroom. We went downstairs to the basement and found JP spray-painting several pairs of sneakers. The room was filled with a haze from the spray paint. Every window was closed. In the next room, the oil burner and the water heater operated on pilot lights. JP was slurring his words and talking about how he wanted to clean up his kicks. The fumes and the pilot light flames easily could have caused an explosion.

A day or two later, we woke up at 3 a.m. to the smell of something burning in the kitchen. JP had attempted to cook and had left a frying pan on the stove with the flame on high. There was a bag of sugar spilled all over the kitchen floor. In the family room, the food he had cooked had fallen off the plate and was mashed into the rug. Joe took JP, who was unsteady on his feet and not making any sense, up to bed.

I got on my hands and knees and began to try to scrape the food off the rug. It was disgusting. I felt like a goddamn fool. I was angry at myself for allowing all of it to go on for as long as it had. Seeing JP so messed up and incoherent— with me following right behind with yet another dustpan and broom to fix a mess—underscored for me how *it was over*.

A dark gift, but a necessary one.

Fate stepped in one afternoon when Mary Ellen, a kind and knowledgeable woman who worked at a rehab facility north of our home, returned a phone call I had left a few days earlier asking to visit the place. She listened patiently and spoke with candor. She did not think that facility was a good fit for JP because so many of the clients were older men with heroin addictions.

"This place is nearby, but it is not the kind of environment you would want to place your son in," she said.

She recommended we look at a treatment center in South Florida, which accepted many insurance programs and had a good reputation for working with young adults. She explained that South Florida offered a lot of post-treatment options while our area did not. Once JP completed treatment, he would need to start his life over in a place without the associations of where he used, she explained. South Florida would offer that. I told her I hadn't even thought of JP being so far away permanently.

"Don't get ahead of yourself," she cautioned. "But keep in mind the big picture long-term is that you want your son in a place where he has support to maintain his sober life."

Her advice was invaluable at the moment when we needed direction we could trust. At that point we knew very little about how to navigate the maze of rehab and recovery program offerings. Not all in-patient rehabs and post-treatment programs are created equal. There are places that are reputable and truly committed to helping an addict recover from the disease of substance abuse. There are also places with terrible track records and practices that are more in the business of profiting from lucrative insurance reimbursements ahead of the needs of the suffering addicts. Mary Ellen's honest guidance helped us tremendously and began the education Joe and I needed about the ins and outs of getting solid help for our son. She truly was an angel in disguise.

We went on the website for the place she recommended, and it looked good. We spoke to a counselor and learned they accepted our insurance. Once JP got on a plane, he would be met at the airport and taken directly to a medical detox to begin treatment. With a plan in place, we were ready to sit down and give JP an ultimatum: agree to go immediately to treatment or leave the house.

But, as we learned the hard way, life sometimes goes terribly off script. That night of confrontation in our kitchen forced us to change our plan.

So be it.

Thus, began nine months of effort in South Florida to help JP get some sober traction, ending with his hasty exit on a bus headed north, flophouse motels, homelessness, and then back to the Y for a second term of residency.

THE
SOLUTION

Chapter 19

"IT'S FUN TO STAY AT THE YMCA" PART II

NANCY

When I was first learning to cook—and there are those who would say I never really *have* learned to cook—my mother humorously taught me a method for determining if spaghetti was done by fishing a piece out of a boiling pot of water and tossing it on the wall. If it stuck to the wall, it was done. If it didn't and fell on the floor, you let the pasta boil a bit more and repeated the toss.

Our efforts with JP felt like my mother's pasta doneness test: we kept throwing solutions at him, hoping one would stick.

And none had.

After years of pasta tossing—imagine the mess on the floor—we were right back to what hadn't worked before: JP living at the YMCA.

The seesawing pattern our family endured for months—emotionally charged confrontations followed by all-too-brief periods where things *seemed to improve*—is a familiar one to those in the throes of this disease. I was lulled into thinking somehow recovery—for all of us—would happen during the seesaw. I wanted to believe that because I personally lacked the courage and conviction to do the very difficult things our circumstances were demanding.

We waited too long.

Parents get caught in the web of where the disease of addiction takes their adult child. I failed to realize over and over that while JP was addicted to substances, *I was addicted to the situation.* Every moment of failure, every moment of (usually false) hope, every problem accompanying the hellish life JP was choosing, I lived to the exclusion of just about everything else.

That was how my life got reduced to delivering crickets to a kindergarten class: I could not separate myself from JP's choices. I allowed myself to be pulled along by the forces of it until I was dangerously far away from the safe compass points of my own existence. My family was both saddened and exasperated by my inability to live life past what JP was doing—or better yet—undoing.

Joe lived with a preoccupied, anxious partner. My daughters saw me tangled in fear, worry, and confusion much of the time. I believed that to be a good mother to JP, I had to live that way.

I was wrong.

There is a 12-step saying: "Let go or be dragged." At some point, I heard it and it resonated. Our oldest daughter, Annie, was very frustrated that we could not let JP deal with the consequences of his choices.

"We're here. He's not. Live your life with us," she would tell me.

Annie was right.

There was a family with a life to be lived, and JP could not be part of that life until he sought help. We all had watched Manzo disappear bit by bit over the years since he started high school. We had hoped stints at the Y, a wilderness program, several detoxes, rehab, assorted halfway houses, and a bunch of other programs I don't even remember would have jump-started a solution.

But they didn't.

It was all a pile of half-cooked spaghetti that didn't stick and fell in a big, hot mess on the floor.

So, when JP relapsed in Florida after about six months of

sobriety and took a Greyhound bus back to New York, I knew it only meant more heart breaking for all of us.

And JP knew that too.

We were resolute enough not to allow JP to move back into our home, and we proceeded with the court case. But when he told us he had a job near the Y, we helped him get a room there *again* by paying his first month's rent. With winter coming on, JP was beaten down enough for the Y to look like a damn good option the second time around.

JP lived at the Y for seven long months. By helping him with the first month's rent, we essentially set up a bunker for him. Of course, we believed we were doing the right thing. But the deeper truth here is I had a *really hard time with a child of mine—even an adult child—being a homeless person.* So, after JP landed back in New York and bounced around sketchy motels and sleeping on floors for six weeks, I had reached my limit for that run of tough love.

Thus, began the Y *Part II*.

As the months passed, JP met all the mandates required by the court. Our interactions with him were infrequent.

In an effort to help the rest of our family through this challenge, our two older daughters, Joe, and I began to meet with Dr. Cipriano weekly, bright and early on Saturday mornings, to discuss how to keep a united front against JP returning home or complicating any of our lives until he sought help. Those sessions were difficult because among the four of us at differing times was a lot of sadness and anger for what had transpired. Looking back on those "Saturday Mornings with Dr. Cip" on the Dysfunctional Family Channel, we each played out a role in the ongoing saga—and that's what families in our situation do. Joe was calm and tried to strike a balance in enforcing tough love with his son. I was generally frantic and desperate on every level. Molly just wanted the brother she remembered to come back and be that great, fun guy again. Annie was the truth teller occupying the *Take No Prisoners Zone*. She was determined not to let anyone welcome back into the fold someone whose actions did not warrant welcome.

We each held a piece of truth, but with the benefit of time I will say that Annie's truth and her very direct manner of delivering it at 8 a.m. (after gulping down one cup of coffee) was probably what I needed most to hear. It was a very clear reminder: there was no room to soften our stance until JP stopped gambling with his life.

Grace was too young to go to these counseling sessions. Just as well. At times they were heated as we each tried to grapple with what had happened. So, Grace would stay home with Annie's boyfriend, Kyle, who generously volunteered to babysit so very early on a weekend morning when he could have slept in. Grace was nonstop energy, and she kept Kyle, who worked hard all week and often went out late with friends on Friday nights, very busy with Legos, board games, cards, DVDs, coloring, food requests, and jumping on the trampoline outside in the cold.

The joke among all of us was that we never could figure out who had the more challenging task on Saturdays—those of us hashing it out in family therapy or Kyle watching Grace.

By the time spring came, JP was working another job as a waiter at a local restaurant. He had lost a lot of weight. His skin was very pale. He looked tired and drained. He called us less frequently and did not ask to see us.

He was slipping away.

There was no anger or threats. He sounded hollow on the phone—as if the life had been sucked out of him. We knew things were getting worse for him. We repeatedly asked him to go to treatment.

He, just as repeatedly, refused.

JP

I was able to get a mixed stash of drugs. Every day before I went into work, I was already high. Before I brushed my teeth, I was high. Before I got dressed, I was high.

I think I was an OK waiter. Whenever there was a customer complaint, I would go in the bathroom, take a pill, and come out and make nice with the customer.

The process of getting high continued every day and every night.

I would go down to New York City and drink. A few of my friends worked at different nightclubs. I would drink heavily at their places.

My room at the YMCA was filled with food, clothes, drug paraphernalia, mice, and cockroaches. At night I would hear the mice moving around, but I never really paid attention to them because I thought I was just hearing things.

The nights that I would go drink in the city, I would get caught up in many dangerous "games." One night I was in a friend's car on the highway, and to be funny I pushed most of my body out the window of the car. Other times, I would open the passenger door and lay with the most of my body outside the car, hanging just over the road, as the car was traveling at a high rate of speed.

I remember seeing my friends' faces as they tried to pull me back in the car. The looked frightened. Even in my highly intoxicated state I remember thinking: What are they so scared about?

I knew what I was doing was dangerous. But I was high and thought it was funny.

NANCY

Dr. Cipriano cautioned us another bottom was looming.

"He is losing hope. He doesn't even believe his own bullshit anymore. No one else does, either."

Grace was to make her First Holy Communion in May. JP is Grace's godfather. It was JP who coaxed a laugh from Grace the day she came home from China. When we arrived after the eighteen-hour flight, there were family members and friends gathered at the house to welcome Grace Rui Rui. There was a big "Welcome Home Rui Rui" sign painted in red on a bedsheet hanging from our front porch with lots of red balloons.

When Grace saw all the unfamiliar faces, she became frightened and started to cry. JP grabbed a few balloons, moved next to Grace, and began to bop himself on the head with the balloons. She stopped crying and started giggling. JP lifted his sister off my lap and made her laugh some more. There was a heart-to-heart bond between them from that instant.

Grace and JP's high-energy levels were well matched. He called her "Little Man." He came to her nursery school and read to her class for her birthday. In the morning, she would climb on his bed and pull his eyelids up to wake him up to come play with her. Together they were an amazing duo.

We planned Grace's First Communion celebration for months—invitations were sent to more than sixty family members and friends. Annie and Molly insisted Grace's dress be full of puffiness, bows, lace, and pearls. JP said he wanted to be with his sister for this important day in her life. He promised he would be at the Mass and the party.

On the morning of the Mass, Joe called JP to tell him to be ready to be picked up. There was no answer. Joe called several more times and then headed over to get him. I was home getting Grace ready in her dress and veil. I felt split down the middle: joy for Grace on her sacramental day and panic that JP was cutting himself off from attending the Mass with all of us.

Where is he? Why isn't he answering the phone? What has happened to him? How can he not show up for Grace?

Joe came back. He didn't say much. The house was bustling with Uncle Bob and his family helping us get ready for lunch after the Mass. Joe took pictures of our three daughters. Waiting at the church were the students I had taught with Grace for a year, preparing them for their First Holy Communion. Everything was in place—except for me. I was occupying two worlds—the one filled with life all around me and the relentless image in my mind of JP passed out on a bed at the Y.

Then came the gift of clarity.

It was a strange gift, really. I sat with my husband and daughters in the church where I had been a member since second grade. I saw our beautiful Grace dressed in white and remembered the frightened little two-year-old with a black eye and bruised face that the orphanage director placed in my arms five years before. I saw all this good surrounding me, and I knew there was no room in it for JP *until he made a choice*.

At the party, Joe made a toast to our Gracie. She spent most of the afternoon jumping on the trampoline in her dress that became as dirty as her play clothes. After all, don't you measure how fun a First Holy Communion party is by the number of dirt and grass stains that wind up on the dress?

At the end of the day, my mentor from Fordham, Sister Janet, came to the house to hand-deliver my diploma because it had also been my graduation day there. It meant a lot to me that this professor, who patiently encouraged me to finish, did this. Holding the diploma in the middle of my kitchen was a reminder that there was a lot of positive momentum in our lives and I needed *to go with the mo*.

JP

A few days prior to my sister Grace receiving her First Holy Communion, there was a dry spell in the drugs I was using. Within a day, I had burned through my stash and was unable to acquire more drugs.

Reality began to set in once again. And so did withdrawal symptoms: sweating, paranoia, hallucinations, and the potential of having a seizure that could have killed me. I was alone in a filthy room at the Y in withdrawal. It continued for two days and got worse and worse.

I planned on going to Grace's First Communion. I come from a Catholic family, and the First Communion is a big deal. And I love my sister.

But when I opened my eyes that morning after the brief stint of sleep I had, I knew there was no way I would be able to go there. And then I envisioned having to speak to family members and friends at the party in the physical shape I was in and the mindset I was in and I knew I would not be capable of any of it. I should have been in a medical detox given what was happening to me physically and mentally.

I knew that it would be better for people not to see me this way. And physically I could not get out of bed.

I wound up not going.

NANCY

JP called me a few days later to explain his absence and I stopped him.

"I don't want to hear any excuses. You did not show up for Grace, your little sister, your own goddaughter. We are done with you, JP. You need professional help. You have an illness. You need to go back to rehab. Let us know when you want help. Otherwise, there is no point in talking. Goodbye."

That was the last we heard from him until the middle of June.

In the intervening weeks, I became very ill one weekend while were working on our summer house to get it ready for renters and was admitted to a hospital in Rhode Island. The three days I spent resting in the hospital gave me a lot of time to reflect on the circus our life had become.

As I was leaving the hospital, my cell phone rang. Annie was calling from New York to tell me my mother had suffered a seizure and was in an ambulance on the way to a hospital. That night Molly told me that while I was in the hospital, JP had to go an emergency room because he had been in a serious accident while "surfing" on top of a moving car.

It was all too much. I could not take one more thing going wrong. My prayers seemed to bounce off some Teflon ceiling in heaven and crash-land on Earth. I asked God to give JP a moment of clarity about his illness of addiction. And hoped that the heavens would crack open enough for my prayer to be heard.

JP

One night I was drinking at a friend's house. I had finished around a thirty-pack of beer by myself. Toward the end of the night, when my friend was leaving, I jumped in front of his car and told him to stop. When he stopped, I laid on the hood of his car and told him to drive fast because I wanted to car surf. He objected at first. But when I began to yell at him to do so, he complied.

Once he hit third gear, I jumped off his car and went flying.

The next thing I remember was being helped off the ground by people who were at the party and heard my crash. I had slid on the asphalt and cracked my head on a stone. I remember everyone having that same scared look on their faces. Several people offered to call 911 and said I needed to go to the hospital.

I told them I would be fine and that I was not going to go to any hospital.

The next morning, I woke up in my dirty, dark room at the Y. The room had blood all over the place, and my pillow was soaked through with blood. When I opened my eyes, it was a very sobering sight.

I quickly called a friend who had always come to my rescue. I told my friend I thought I had lost a lot of blood and needed to go to the hospital.

The doctor ordered a CAT scan. I remember the doctor and the nursing staff looking at me like I was crazy and asking me how I sustained such an injury to my head. I told them I was riding on a dirt bike and crashed. They had to clean the road rash off my back and arms that had ripped apart the layers of clothing I was wearing.

Throughout this time there were a few brief moments when I was sober. During those small seconds of sobriety, I felt anxiety, pain, depression, self-hatred, and morbid thoughts. But, most importantly, in those brief moments, there was a *deep yearning* in my true self to stop living this way. Very deep inside of all that pain, anger, and detrimental behavior was the real me who wanted to be positive, happy, and have relationships with loved ones.

Chapter 20

A FATHER'S DAY DEAL

NANCY

I was waiting for God to answer some prayers.

Father's Day was a few days after I got home from the hospital. The girls and I gave Joe presents and cards, and we all had breakfast and dinner together. No one spoke of JP. We just enjoyed Joe's special day.

After dinner, a powerful thunderstorm blew in. It was almost 10 p.m. when we heard a knock at the front door. There in the glass window standing soaking wet was JP.

I knew, just as sure as I knew my own name, that his arrival was the answer to prayer.

He said he wanted to talk to us. He didn't want to come in the house. He asked us to join him outside on the stone porch in the front of the house.

It was very dark out, and the rain was coming down in sheets. The three of us sat together on white wicker chairs, sheltered by the big porch roof held up by 100-year-old fieldstone walls and columns as thunder crashed overhead. Somehow it felt safe for all of us.

Even in the darkness, I could see JP was thin and broken.

"I need help," he said in a soft voice. "I can't do this anymore. I don't want to go to rehab. I've done that already. I know what I need to do. I just want to go to detox and back to meetings."

A negotiation of sorts ensued. Joe and I knew our end game was to get JP back to Florida with the sober support network for him there. JP wasn't buying that. But we would work with any willingness he demonstrated with the hope that once he was in a therapeutic environment, he would agree to stay for treatment.

The deal we brokered with JP that night was for him to go to detox at the Florida rehab where he had completed treatment before. If he decided after detox that he did not want to stay for further help, we would get him a plane ticket home.

At that moment, it was the best we could do.

We were banking on the *if*. We were going to play this out *as if* JP would decide to stay after detox. We called Paul to tell him JP was coming down for detox but wanted to return to New York once it was done.

"OK. Just get him down here tomorrow. We'll deal with it. I'll talk to him. We'll get this going. Don't worry."

JP

I don't remember showing up at my parents' house to ask for help. But I do remember the feelings that I had right before going to detox again. I had come to the realization that my life was falling apart.

I had not taken drugs or alcohol for a couple of days, so a window into the pain, anguish, and heartache I was running from started to open. Without the substances in my body, the reality of everything that had taken place started to set in. I had raw emotions. My nerves felt like I was having teeth drilled without novocaine.

Back then I prided myself on not crying and not showing my emotions. And I cried for a good three hours before I got on the plane. The general state that I was in was broken. It was like the foundation of a house that has been demolished. Little remained of who I had once been years before.

I was empty and drained. I knew that when I was in Florida before, I had been sober for a period of time, and although I really didn't do shit to stay sober, there was a part of me there that was alive. I wanted to get in touch with that part of me again.

But I wanted to do things *my* way—even though, as evidenced by the last two years, my way obviously didn't work. I still wanted to do things my way. I thought I knew best.

I wound up making a deal with my parents and going to Florida for detox.

NANCY

It was very late, and we needed to move quickly. We called the treatment center, arranged for a bed in the detox, worked out the finances, and booked a flight for the next morning.

Like an O. Henry story, Father's Day ended with an unexpected twist: our son showing up at the door with some willingness. Joe responded to his son's request for help with unconditional love—the essence of Father's Day, really, a tremendous gift.

As I lay in bed in the dark with the storm outside and my husband and all four of my children safely inside, I felt a lot of gratitude—another unexpected gift—for answered prayer.

The next morning, JP did not want to get out of bed.

Nothing new here.

The clock was running down on getting him to the airport and through security in time for his plane. Joe had jobs in the city, so I was left to get this done. With less than two hours until the flight, JP finally got up and showered—in a leisurely manner. I began to think this whole plan was a bad idea. That feeling intensified when JP asked to use the car to go buy cigarettes.

I started to feel anxious, and as the minutes ticked by, the anxiety ratcheted into panic. JP was gone for almost twenty minutes and we were now late to get to the airport. When he walked in the door, he looked high.

Great.

Molly and Grace wanted to go to the airport with their brother. We arrived with just about ten minutes to spare. The security lines were long, and I knew JP would miss the plane if I didn't do something fast. I grabbed him by the arm and ran to the TSA officer at the front of the line.

"My son needs to be on the plane to Palm Beach that is

boarding now. He has a medical situation. There are people waiting for him when he arrives. You need to let him go through."

The TSA officer was no dummy. He could hear the panic in my voice and see that JP was a sloppy mess. He agreed to let him jump the line. We watched the plane take off.

It was a beautiful early summer afternoon. JP had blown in like an errant wind for less than twenty-four hours. My good friend, Kathy, has a saying: "Everything always looks better after an ice cream cone." There are times when that's a powerfully good idea.

"What do you say girls; I think this calls for some ice cream on the way home?"

Agreed.

JP was in detox for five days. Paul went to see him there. He tried to talk JP into staying for treatment. The staff at the treatment center all spoke to him too, but no one could crack his resolve. On the night before he was to be discharged, JP called and asked us to buy him a ticket back. Joe and I wanted to say, "Tough luck. Stay in Florida. Help is there for you."

But we knew we had to act with integrity and keep our end of the deal—even if our plan had backfired. We picked JP up at the airport twenty-four hours later.

We decided to let JP stay at our house instead of going back to the Y for at least one more night. I was still holding onto the hope lightning would strike and JP would decide to go to a Florida halfway house with Paul. We had dinner together. JP went to a meeting and came right home.

A hopeful sign.

The next day began well enough. In the kitchen over coffee, JP told me how desperate his life had become. I was surprised by his honesty. He wanted to see his medical doctor, and we headed up to his office. After lunch he asked me to go to the Eucharistic Adoration chapel with him to pray. As we walked over to the church, JP took my arm. It was a tender act, something he hadn't done for a long time. He sat there in the silence of the chapel before the monstrance holding the Holy Eucharist for a while. As we walked back home, he took my arm again and the truth came spilling out.

"I need to get out of here, Mom. I can't do this here. I need to go back to Florida. I've been lying to you. I drank on the plane ride home from detox. I love you. I love being home. I thought I could do this, but I need to leave."

"OK, JP, we will get you on a plane tomorrow morning."

"No, Mom, you don't understand. I need to leave today. Right away."

He had been home for less than twenty-four hours. It was all moving too fast. But I didn't care. JP was now willing to take his situation seriously. I called Joe.

JP was sitting in the living room alone, and he began sobbing.

"My life is a mess. I've ruined my life. I've ruined everything," he repeated over and over.

Annie heard his sobbing and came downstairs. She was as stunned as I was to see JP crying. I tried to comfort him while Annie got on the computer to purchase a plane ticket. JP's whole body was shaking as he continued to cry. I began to get worried that he was having some kind of breakdown. I called Joe again and told him JP was in a precarious emotional state and that he would need to go down on the plane with him. And, bless that man, Joe agreed.

By now Annie had found two seats on a flight leaving John F. Kennedy Airport in three hours. It was nearing rush hour and the airport was more than an hour away. I was really getting concerned about JP's stability because he was still sobbing.

The only person I knew who could help JP at that exact moment was Paul. I took the phone outside on the front porch and called him. He could hear the fear in my voice as I described how JP was sobbing uncontrollably.

"I've never seen him like this, Paul. Maybe I should take him to a hospital."

"OK, Nance, let me talk to him. Please put him on the phone for a minute," he said calmly.

JP sat outside on the porch, and for twenty minutes Paul talked to him. Gradually, he began to regain his composure.

JP handed me the phone.

"OK. Nancy, he is going to get on the plane with Joe. He will be all right. I will meet Joe and JP at the airport. This is a good thing, Nancy. He is coming back. Just get him on the plane."

There are amazing people whose mission on earth is to help others. I don't mean to get all celestial, but I think God whispers special instructions in their tiny, infant ears as they are sent from heaven to earth to begin to fulfill their destinies at birth. Their hearts have extra chambers to embrace difficult, complicated situations with more than the usual measure of love, constancy, wisdom, and humor. Life has richly blessed our family with these amazing friends and mentors. That evening —as was the case so many times before and many still to come—that amazing person was Paul.

Joe got home, threw some stuff in a bag, and started to drive at a high rate of speed to the airport. There was a lot of traffic out to JFK. But somehow Joe and JP arrived on time to make the plane.

JP

I spent five days down in Florida in detox, and on the flight back I drank, which is kind of crazy being that I had just completed detox and began to drink minutes after leaving there.

But I didn't think much of it.

Benzo withdrawals sometimes don't start for a week, and that definitely happened in my case. The withdrawals started kicking in, and I was out of my mind.

This withdrawal was much harder than I remembered from the times before.

I kept thinking I was going to make it work. But to be honest, my mental state scared even me. It was like I was in a panic and alarms were going off in my head.

Within three hours of being home after my mom got me at the airport, I had gone and picked up drugs. I knew it wasn't going to work being home.

I felt so spaced out that nothing felt real. I remember thinking that life was so surreal it felt like a video game.

Once I got home, I went to my family doctor to get a check-up with my mom.

I told my mom I could drive, which was probably a bad idea. My mom let me drive at first and then told me I was veering to the wrong side of the street. I didn't think I was. My whole sense of perception was distorted.

Outside the doctor's office, I called my friend and told him I would need some prescription medication for that night. I didn't like the way I felt, and I knew using would make that go away.

In the back of my mind, I knew this was wrong. But I didn't know any other way to make this horrible feeling go away. I kept the pills I purchased earlier in the day in my pocket. There was a part of me that knew I shouldn't take them. And I didn't.

Later my mom and I went to church. Right afterward I told my mother I needed to get back to Florida to get sober. I felt like a failure. It was a sign of defeat for me to go back to Florida. My parents were fearful that something would happen to me and booked a flight for a few hours later.

My pride, my ego, my sense of self-reliance was out the window. I was starting to realize I could not stop on my own. This was a very grave realization for the guy who for the longest time denied ever being a drug addict or an alcoholic. I broke down and was flooded with both anger and sadness. I cried for two hours nonstop, and back then I prided myself on being someone who doesn't cry, which in hindsight was a bunch of bullshit bravado—but I still believed it then. What was happening was everything that I was running from and all the feelings I had numbed suddenly became very real and apparent.

I spoke to my closest sober friend, Paul, and asked him if he could make room for me at the halfway house he was running. He could hear my voice strained and cracking. He outlined how much better I could feel and what could possibly be waiting for me in Florida, if I did the right thing.

Before I got in the car to the airport, I gulped down the pills I had in my pocket. My father was accompanying me on the plane. While we were waiting to board, I had the audacity to ask my father to buy me a drink—I guess the pills had kicked in. He said he wouldn't and seemed really annoyed. I then went over to the bar and ordered two extra-strong Long Island Iced Teas. They were both finished within a few minutes.

I remember walking back over to the gate where everyone was waiting to board the plane. I must have been very loud and obnoxious, and I remember my father looking at me like I was nuts.

I got on the plane back to Florida. Paul met me at the airport.

NANCY

After we dropped off Joe and JP, I took Grace to her first evening of Vacation Bible School at a local church. VBS is a beautiful way to welcome summer—lots of Bible stories, crafts, snacks, and hymns. Someone took a picture of Grace and me arriving at the church. In the picture, we are wearing matching dresses and Grace is leaning up against me, both of us smiling. The picture is now in a frame in my bedroom. It captures a moment I treasure, for the obvious—Grace and I at the opening night of VBS— and for the unspoken, the gratitude knowing JP was in a safe place finally choosing to get help.

As I saw all those young children arrive at the church, I thought of the days since Father's Day: decisions, deals, pain, and now a little green, growing hope. I thanked God for that patch of green. I prayed for traveling mercies for Joe and JP. I thanked God for my family and for Paul. And I thanked God for the sweet little voices I heard singing songs about Jesus in a chapel on a summer's night.

Chapter 21

NOTHING CHANGES IF NOTHING CHANGES

NANCY

Back in Florida, JP moved into a halfway house run by Paul. He found a job and made some moves to take a class to prepare for a high school equivalency exam. We went to visit him in late August before everyone returned to school. JP received permission to stay with us instead of coming back to the halfway house at night. We all mashed into a very small hotel room together.

No one took this time for granted. Instead of it being an inconvenience to be in one room, we joked about who got stuck sleeping on the cot, who snored, and who hogged the towels. We ate meals together as a family. We took the family Christmas card picture on a balcony overlooking the Atlantic Ocean. The water in South Florida is like a bathtub in late August, and all six of us spent a few days at the beach sunning, playing chicken fights and Marco Polo together.

Then we piled in the car and headed to Disney for the second part of the trip, where Annie's boyfriend, Kyle, met us. The rental car was way too small to fit all seven of us. That got us all laughing too. Our three days at Disney were terrific. When we said goodbye to JP, everyone's outlook was positive, and we made plans for him to come home over Columbus Day weekend.

JP

I really did want to get sober. I had tried to make it work on my own terms for the past nine months and had failed. I now felt the harsh realities of my substance abuse problem. I was miserable. I hadn't accomplished anything or done anything positive in more than two years. It was time for me to change.

I was already familiar with what I needed to do from the last time I was in Florida, which I didn't do then. I needed to get a sponsor, go to 12-step meetings, and work a program. In layman's terms, these actions basically consist of becoming honest, taking ownership for your wrongs, trying to right your wrongs by living in a positive way, and helping other people.

It sounds pretty simple, but in the mindset of someone in early recovery, it can be a daunting task. And it was for me.

I thought by returning to Florida and just hanging around people who worked solid 12-step programs, I would get sober through osmosis.

I was wrong.

I spent the next few weeks socializing, lighting fireworks, not working, and socializing some more. I was more interested in meeting women, making friends, and earning a reputation—a bad one at that— than working the suggested program of recovery.

This was a prime example of me doing things *my way*. The mess I had made of my life doing things on my own terms was evidence enough that I don't know what the hell I was thinking. The fact is: *I wasn't thinking; my addiction was.*

Although I wasn't yet feeding my addiction by using substances, it was still very active while it played possum, firing off different delusions and distortions.

My lack of effort and sloth continued for a while.

My family came down within a few months to see me. In hindsight, I am not sure why they came down. I was full of excuses and was not doing a goddamn worthwhile thing. But I expected to get credit for this non-effort and believed I was doing a great job doing absolutely nothing with my life. Back then, I often believed my own bullshit.

I had a nice vacation with my family. After they left, I decided my tremendous effort to get sober—which in reality was no effort at all—was enough. Within a few days, I thought it would be a good idea to get high. I decided it was time to try to use successfully again by using drugs on a limited basis and somehow controlling the outcome.

I remember thinking on a Sunday, "I will get high tonight and that's it. Just tonight."

That same thought process continued on Monday, Tuesday, Wednesday, and Thursday. On Thursday I remember thinking, "Holy shit how did this happen? It was only supposed to be one day."

I knew that I had a drug test coming up on Friday. I knew that if I stopped getting high, I would get sick from withdrawals. I then got together with two buddies from the halfway house and devised a plan to move into an apartment. We moved out of the halfway house into an apartment with no electricity and no furniture.

I didn't eat for about a week and a half. I remember patches of that period of time when I lived in that apartment, but most of what I remember is a blur, a miserable blur.

I wound up in another detox. I got out of there and went to another halfway house. I was then kicked out of that halfway house for using.

NANCY

The plans to see JP at Columbus Day never materialized. We received phone calls from him; he promised that he was sober and doing well. But that was a lie. A week or so later, JP called, asking us to get him into detox. We spoke to Paul. He told us not to pay for another detox stint for JP.

"Don't you spend another dime on some nice place for him. He can go to a state-run detox. It's disgusting there. Let him see where he is going to end up."

We followed Paul's suggestion.

In late November, Paul said JP seemed to be on a good path and there was a decent chance we could spend a few days at Christmas with him. We all put our heads together for a way to see JP, but keep him out of the harm's way of old associations at home. We came up with a plan to spend Christmas at our beach house in Rhode Island. JP could fly in to Providence on Christmas Eve and fly back to Florida on December 27.

Our daughters weren't exactly in love with the idea of being there for Christmas. But they understood this was the best way to ensure we could all be together. My mother and aunt kindly agreed to change their plans and join us there.

Over Thanksgiving weekend, we went up to Rhode Island with a couple of boxes of Christmas decorations to get ready. We decorated the house with a little artificial Christmas tree and put up a Nativity set in the living room. We even bought a special golden key for Grace to leave out for Santa on Christmas Eve, so he could enter our home because there is no fireplace there for him to climb down.

Joe bought JP's plane tickets. We talked to him frequently on the phone. He kept saying how much he wanted to come home. I felt hope that Christmas would be a homecoming for our son.

At the end of the first week of December, Paul called.

"JP failed a drug test. He's left the house. I don't know where he is."

JP

I got another apartment with two of my friends and continued to use there. For the first seventy-two hours of living there, there was no electricity.

I had asked a kid from the halfway house where I was living if I could borrow his car for an hour. The following morning, I was greeted by someone telling me the police were about to arrive because the kid had filed a report that I had stolen the car.

I told them that they could take the car and said some sort of insult to the kid who owned it. Later that day, I was asked to leave work, due to the fact, that I couldn't keep my eyes open.

The following two weeks were a blur. I was living in a blackout. I was using everything under the sun. I was now using from the second I opened my eyes till the second my eyes were closed.

If I had thought the "toxic mixes" I was on in the past were bad, this was worse. I was taking Ecstasy, Xanax, Oxycodone, and Ambien, along with alcohol and anything else I could get my hands on. I wound up getting so bad that my two friends who were getting high with me said I had to leave.

I wasn't eating because I didn't want to cut down on the potency of the drugs I was using by ingesting food. When I took drugs, I didn't shoot them. In my mind, when they were sitting in my stomach, the food would absorb some of them and waste them. Not eating was a bonus from a monetary standpoint and a junkie standpoint. I dropped fifteen pounds in two weeks.

When people saw me, they would say "Wow!" or "Oh my God; you are so skinny!" In my distorted mind, I took it as a compliment—that they were saying I looked good. They were actually saying that I looked unhealthy, that I was eerily skinny and ghostly white.

In the mind of an active addict, anything that doesn't directly have to do with consuming drugs or ways to get drugs is irrelevant and doesn't resonate in the brain for long.

After getting kicked out of the halfway house, checking into another detox, and getting kicked out of the apartment, I got into another halfway house and decided to use again. I craved drugs. If I had any idle time, the thought would pop into my head within seconds about how nice it would be to use.

Within a few weeks, I was kicked out of that halfway house. I then got a room at a crack motel.

Chapter 22

A CHRISTMAS GIFT OF ACCEPTANCE

NANCY

Throughout Advent while JP was living in a crack motel, my spiritual director, Sister Kathleen, encouraged me to read the Gospel of Luke's Infancy Narratives with an eye toward the uncertainty surrounding Mary and Joseph's future as they traveled to Bethlehem. It was an uphill climb for the Holy Family: an unplanned pregnancy, the decision Joseph faced over whether to stay with Mary, their search for a birthing place for Jesus, and their flight to Egypt to escape Herod's murderous wrath.

It was comforting to read the familiar words and food for the soul in considering the Holy Family's difficult circumstances. Of course, there were a few battalions of heavenly angels and a prophetic dream or two thrown in the mix to encourage and guide Mary and Joseph along the way. Joe and I were back to being insomniacs, so we weren't receiving much in the way of prophetic dreams.

But in keeping with the gospel theme that God provides us with what we need on our journeys, a good friend who has a direct-hit approach of conveying the truth told me what I needed to hear.

"Your three daughters, your husband, and you deserve to have Christmas even if JP doesn't. Sometimes things can't be tied up in a neat bow. It just has to all hang out and be a mess, and at some point, it will get resolved."

Her words snapped me into some clear thinking. I redoubled my efforts to stick to the script of our family's Christmas traditions. I plastered a smile on my face and whipped up egg whites to make royal frosting for building gingerbread houses. We put up the tree, wrapped presents, and baked slice-and-bake (OK, we cheated a little) cookies.

Ho ho ho.

JP was calling every few days, telling us it was Christmas, he was homeless, and we needed to send him some money. We weren't doing that. The phone calls were brief. He was desperate. When he called on his twenty-first birthday, it was hard to say no. But we did.

Paul called me later the same day with a message I needed to hear. And with the benefit of time, I realize that message from Paul was one of the most important of my life. Now when I speak with other parents struggling with their adult child's addiction, I often share this conversation in the hope it will help them as much as it helped me.

"Nancy, listen to me. You cannot under any circumstances send him money. No matter what. No matter whether it's Christmas or not. It doesn't matter. If he tells you he is starving, you say no.

"Nancy, I knew a kid, he begged his mother to wire him twenty bucks, just twenty bucks so he could get something to eat. The mother listened to her son. She believed she was doing the right thing. She wired him the money. He went and bought drugs with it, and that night he died of an overdose.

"She has to live with that for the rest of her life. For the rest of her life, Nancy. She has to live with the fact that she provided money for the drugs that killed her son.

"Nancy, you are a loving mother, right? You want to be a loving mother to your son, right?"

"Yes, Paul that's what I want to be. I want to love JP," I answered, crying.

"You need to walk away. You need to leave him and let him hit his bottom. That is how you can love your son. That is the most loving thing you can do—walk the hell away. He needs to find this for himself. There is nothing more you can do for him right now.

"There is nothing more any of us can do for him."

Paul's words hit me like a two-by-four across the face.

But after the pain of contact came clarity. Paul's words gave me the resolve and the context I needed to take the drastic but absolutely necessary action of no action.

This is how to love JP—by walking away.

We had exhausted every possible solution. It was rock hard, but it made sense. Paul had put it in the only context I could really understand: walking away was the most loving thing to do.

Christmas or not, this was the only choice.

With JP hundreds of miles away, a strung-out voice on random phone calls, Joe and I were both feeling a sense of mounting desperation. We knew this was not going to end well. And we were back to speaking shorthand in the middle of the night.

"Joe, what if...?"

"Nancy, no matter what. We have done *everything* we could."

JP

I continued to use drugs in the room at the crack motel. I was miserable. Getting high was no longer fun. As a matter of fact, the potency of the "fun" had started to dwindle a long time before. I was ingesting a small pharmacy, and I was numb and in a blackout most of the time. I finally realized that I wasn't going to be able to continue this way much longer.

I could almost feel my soul leaving my body.

And I was really close to dying.

NANCY

Once again, I knew I could not comfortably attend Christmas Eve Mass at our parish. My uncle, Father Luke, was living at a nearby Catholic nursing home because he was suffering from Alzheimer's and Parkinson's diseases. I enjoyed going to Mass with my him and his full-time aide, Mr. Emmanuel. My uncle, who earned a half dozen master's degrees and a doctorate in English literature from Columbia University, had been a brilliant homilist. But now he suffered severe limitations physically and cognitively. But he was still able to attend Mass in a wheelchair and quietly whisper prayers still resting in his memory.

Going to Christmas Eve Mass with my uncle was a good alternative and a way to give back to him for the many, many years he had been such a powerful spiritual and an intellectual force in my life. I guess I was seeking some sort of *connection* with my uncle to help me deal with what was happening.

It didn't quite turn out that way.

Molly agreed to go with me to the nursing home to the "First Mass of Christmas"—held at 11 a.m. When we arrived, my uncle wasn't there. We decided to visit him after Mass. The chapel was filled with morning sunlight, red poinsettias, and joy as row after row of elderly residents and their families sang carols and prayed together.

When Mass ended, we took the elevator to my uncle's floor, and as we stepped out, we heard a man's voice screaming loudly. We walked into his room to find him lying in his bed, arms and legs thrashing. He had a terrified look in his eyes, as if some unseen force in the room was tormenting him. Mr. Emmanuel stood next to him, trying calm him down.

I tried to take my uncle's hand. He pushed it away.

"I didn't want you to see Father Luke like this," Mr. Emmanuel said. "It's not your uncle here, Nancy."

He gently directed us out to the hallway.

Something snapped. It was a pileup really: all the months of watching JP unravel, fearing that he would die, feeling so completely off-kilter with Joe, handling my mother's illnesses and Grace's vision problems, and now seeing my uncle so compromised. I began to cry, and I couldn't stop.

There was just so much damage all around. Damage that couldn't be fixed, no matter how hard I tried. Then I realized that crying in front of my daughter outside my uncle's room wasn't going to solve a damn thing. I went into a bathroom and washed my face with cold water. After that I didn't cry again for a long time.

We kept to all our family's traditions on Christmas Day. We opened gifts and shared a big breakfast in the dining room, with quiches and baked ham. I tried to push away any disturbing images of JP homeless. I forced myself to keep Paul's words in the forefront of my mind.

JP called late in the afternoon. We told him we would call him back from the phone in Joe's office in the converted barn next to our home. We did not want our daughters to overhear any difficult conversation with him.

Joe's office was cold, and it was getting dark. We didn't turn the lights on. We were completely alone with JP on speakerphone. I felt like I was in some kind of tomb with the disembodied voice of my son.

He asked us to wire thirty dollars to a bodega.

"I don't have the money to give you. When you want help to stop using drugs, please contact us and we will help you get to rehab," Joe said in a steady voice.

"How can you say no to me? It's Christmas. I'm your son. I am hungry. I have nothing to eat."

"No, JP, we can't do this for you. We are praying for you. We will help you when you are ready to get help for your addiction," Joe said. "We love you, remember that."

JP ended the phone call quickly. There was really nothing more for any of us to say. But having gotten over that hurdle on Christmas Day, I knew it would make the next request easier to refuse.

I had to surrender to my own powerlessness many, many times over the course of this journey. But that day I held a huge white flag in my hand—a tattered one at that. I was such a slow learner when it came to *powerlessness*, which Joe pretty much had mastered all along.

Paul's words, Joe's stance, and Uncle Luke's illness were the Christmas angels—angels dressed in somber robes—but angels nonetheless because they led me to the part of the

Serenity Prayer I always wrestled with: "to accept the things I cannot change."

Throughout this time, the story of Jacob wrestling with God in the Book of Genesis attracted me because it is such a hard-core account of powerful good being born out of exhaustion and struggle. Jacob was a cunning, even ruthless man who had cheated his own brother, Esau, out of his inheritance. At one point in the story, Jacob heads toward a showdown with his brother, who has planned to kill him.

He is alone in the desert with no protection, and there he encounters a mysterious angelic figure with whom he wrestles through the night until daybreak. Jacob is a fighter. He won't give up. But the figure outmaneuvers him, winning this physical combat against Jacob by dislocating the socket of his thigh.

Dawn is breaking. The figure tells Jacob, who is now disabled, to let go. But Jacob will have none of it.

"I will not let you go unless you bless me."

The mysterious figure bestows a blessing on Jacob with a new name.

"Your name shall no longer be Jacob, but Israel, because you have struggled with God and with humans and have overcome" (Gn 32:7-29).

Thereafter, Jacob walked with a limp for the rest of his life. It was *in the injury* that the conversion took place. It was *in the struggle* that his new identity was forged. He was a changed man. He recognized the encounter was with God, and his soul was changed.

I love Jacob because he was so fabulously flawed. He fought to the end without even recognizing he was in the ring with a big-time, spiritual heavyweight. Cornered, injured, exhausted, he had the temerity to insist on a blessing, which turned his life around and led to the new destiny God truly intended for him. The story of Jacob's combat first came to my attention during a Protestant church service almost two decades before. A female minister preached on the passage and shared a profound struggle in her own life and how Jacob and his struggle companioned her throughout. The minister was a slender young woman with flaming red hair who could be seen wearing black leather pants when she wasn't in ministerial robes.

These many years later, I can still relive the moment of when I heard her preach about Jacob's struggle and how it mirrored her own. It was inspiring to see a woman preach so eloquently about her own lived experience and how this down-and-dirty Old Testament story had enlightened her. The image of relentless Jacob crippled and then reborn through his physical and spiritual injury, powered my appreciation of the sometimes very rough and circuitous road we flawed human beings must travel to encounter God.

That Sunday in the church, when JP was an adorably rambunctious two-year-old, was a gift on many levels. And the staying power of Jacob's story shared by a woman of faith from a pulpit was a comfort to me on Christmas Day almost twenty years later when JP was homeless. There were years of Jacob in me and there were years of Jacob in JP, each fighting it out with God. Each of us blind to the blessing the struggle would birth.

That Christmas Day I was done wrestling, which immediately moved my chip on the game board a lot closer to HOME for all of us. As with Jacob, the hard-fought blessing was on its way. We didn't see it then, but something was about to be born. A new destiny was about to unfold. But the unfolding demanded we meet a harsh condition by cutting JP completely loose.

Joe and I sat together in silence after JP got off the phone. Given that it was Christmas evening and most families were deep into ribbons, wrappings, and twinkling tree lights, it was a strange moment. The winter sky was getting dark. We were alone in a cold office after cutting off our son. Miles away, JP was alone left to deal with the burden of his choices. We went back to our house to be with our daughters.

Chapter 23

THE PRODIGAL SON'S MOM AND DAD

NANCY

On New Year's Day I ran into Evelyn, my first newspaper editor, at an event. She was bureau chief in an office that had a fraternity house vibe. Evelyn and the guys had coined a nickname for me: Nanny McCanny. I wanted to put on a happy face for Evelyn, but she is not someone you can fool. Instead I told her my son was a homeless addict. Evelyn did not address JP's situation. She simply said, "Nanny, remember who you are. Remember who you are."

Remember who you are.

Her words cut through the failure and self-loathing I was wrapped in.

Remember who you are.

I thanked her. It was sound advice I needed to hear from a good friend on the first day of a New Year.

JP resurfaced that afternoon and—no surprises here—he found a halfway house to take him. He called us on the phone as we were driving to Manhattan with our daughters. He gave us the name and phone of the manager of the halfway house, who said they would do a great job supervising our son's sobriety and would we send a check for $800 to cover the cost of processing his application?

We strongly felt this halfway house and JP's promises were not truthful. But we agreed to fund it in the hopes he would make good on his word to stay clean. We knew from

Paul that all halfway houses were not created equal. In fact, some are what I call puppy mills—places that house kids still using so they can collect the weekly rent for a bed. Our sense was this place was a puppy mill.

Right after we got off the phone with JP, we called Paul and asked him about the place. Paul bluntly described it as a dump run by dishonest people.

"But that's ok," he said, matter of factly. "He's not going to last long there. He will wind up using and being thrown out, and that will help him reach his bottom. It's a terrible place."

OK.

If I could rewind the tape, it would have been wiser to insist JP find a "Paul-approved" place to live or sleep on the beach with other homeless people. It would have shortened the dangling by a noose we were all doing by going along with a sham.

JP

I reached out to my parents and told them I was sober. I asked them to help me get into another halfway house, and they agreed. I actually had been sober for a few days and remember thinking: I have to stop this negative cycle.

A few days later, a guy offered me drugs. It didn't take much convincing and off again I went. My usage reignited like a keg filled with gunpowder. I almost instantaneously surpassed where I had left off and the amount I was using.

This is the unfortunate reality of drug addiction. When addicts stop using for a day, a month, or a year, the disease still remains exactly where it was since the last time. Shortly after they relapse and re-ingest whatever substances, they are right back to where they left off.

I continued to use at this halfway house for the remainder of my time there.

NANCY

The story of the Prodigal Son in the Gospel of Luke began to take on a deeper meaning for me. Church can be such a cleaned-up experience. I love the language of this parable; it is not cleaned up at all. The younger son had been living a low-life existence. He was a heartless, selfish young man who demanded his share of his father's inheritance before his father even died. A fellow of this caliber probably isn't occupying a church pew on Sunday.

This more than two-thousand-year-old story offers a model for how families can recover. The father completely cut his son loose when he demanded his share of the family inheritance. The father did so without anger or recrimination. He left the burden of the son's decision fully on his son.

The son left for a "distant country, and there squandered his wealth in wild living." Now the father was a man of some means with a lot of options. He could have sent a family emissary to track down his lost boy. He could have gone in person to try to persuade his wayward adult child of the error of his ways. He could have gone rogue and sent a goon squad to knock some sense into the son.

But the father did none of these things—he waited.

How did he do that? How did he hold off from worrying, seeking, enabling, hunting, or railing against his son?

Those are all things I did.

But based on Luke's spare prose, the father had a far different and far more effective strategy. This strategy can be seen when the broken son finally journeyed home.

"But while he was still a long way off, his father saw him and was filled with compassion for him; he ran to his son, threw his arms around him and kissed him" (Lk 15:20).

I envision the father as being on the lookout—every single day—for his son's return. I imagine he had a vantage point with sweeping views of the roads leading home where he would go daily and hold a place of hope in his heart for his son. I see the father as standing sentinel at that vantage point daily—maybe even a couple of times a day—praying for his son's homecoming.

Now Luke gives us no clue as to what went on with the father interiorly. Maybe he was pissed off at his son; maybe he did worry; maybe he wracked his brains over how things could have gone differently.

But ultimately, the father's waiting stance bore fruit and his heart was fully ready to receive his son *in God's time*. The father waited and prayed when there was not a shred of evidence the son would ever return. And I believe those fatherly prayers helped the wayward son realize eating pig slop was not a good life strategy. That image of the waiting father was a source of encouragement for me as I waited for JP's homecoming. I just wished I could have waited with as much grace as I envision that father had.

Safe to say, my husband, Joe, has a lot more of the father's character and temperament in him than I do. I admire Joe deeply. My husband's ability to distance himself from JP's choices and to accept with some degree of peace events that were unfolding—even if it wasn't what he ever wanted for his son—proved a much better way of managing the whole thing than my pretty much chronically frantic stance.

Who knows? Maybe there was a Mother of the Prodigal Son home wringing her hands in a state of high anxiety about her son's situation. Maybe that's why the father went alone to the vantage point to look for his lost son—because the Mother of the Prodigal Son was just pretty damn crazed by the whole thing and difficult to live with. Maybe she spent a lot of her time complaining about the whole situation to the older brother. (Maybe that's one of the reasons why the older brother had such resentment about his younger brother.)

And what did the Mother of the Prodigal Son do to keep it together while her younger son unraveled, and her husband waited?

Now that's something to ponder . . .

Chapter 24

JAIL AND GOD'S HAND

NANCY

We heard very little from JP once he got into the puppy mill-halfway house. And we left it that. The fact that he had a roof over his head and was being drug tested was a good thing—at least for the time being. The late winter weeks passed uneventfully. We stuck to the script: "No news is good news." We knew it would be short lived. I made up my mind to enjoy living the day in front of me and not peering frantically into the future for *whatever* lay ahead.

In early March, Joe went up to Rhode Island one Saturday to work on the house. I spoke to Joe later that day, and in an exasperated tone, he told me that he was busy trying to fix a leak from a frozen pipe that had flooded our kitchen and dining room floors. He called in the evening to say he hadn't been able to get it fixed, needed to get more plumbing supplies when the stores opened in the morning, and would be home later Sunday afternoon.

At around 10 p.m., my three daughters and I were all sitting in the living room when the phone rang. The number on the caller ID showed a Florida area code. I answered. It was a collect call from JP. He told me he had been arrested and was in jail. He said he had spoken to Joe earlier in the day and Joe had told him he wanted nothing to do with him. JP asked me to help him. Then the phone went dead.

My entire body started shaking. I asked Grace to leave the room. I called Joe in RI, and he confirmed that JP had called him that afternoon from the jail.

"*What?* You just left him there?"

"Yes. Nancy, he needs to learn a lesson. Let him figure this out."

"Joe, we've got to do something!"

"I'm up here. He's down there in jail. He can take care of this himself."

I understood Joe's point—on one level.

But the other level—the out-of-my-mind-mother level—wanted to make sure he was not in some dire situation.

I called Paul.

"OK, Nancy. You have got to calm down. I will swing by and see what's going on. Don't worry. This is a good thing. This was going to happen. Now it has, and hopefully this will push him to do the right thing."

I was hammered with fear. But I did hear one thing right—Paul said, "swing by." Those are surprisingly easygoing words for someone on the way to a local jail. You swing by Starbucks. You swing by a friend's house. You do not swing by a jail to check on someone's son. In a rational part of my mind, I knew Paul was trying to reassure me.

I held onto the phrase "swing by" and hoped Paul could straighten it out.

JP

There were a lot of messes and headaches while I lived at this halfway house. I wound up drinking and using heavily one night with other house residents. In the morning I was woken up by one of the house managers, who told me the police were on their way for me and to leave immediately. I told him to go fuck himself and went back to sleep. Due to my behavior during the previous evening, I was greeted by four police officers and escorted off the property in handcuffs.

I called my father from jail. He said he had no interest in speaking to me and that he was not going to help me. While sitting in the jail cell, I remember thinking that this was going to be a new reality of my life and that I needed to get used to this happening.

The fact is that while I was using drugs, I was committing

numerous crimes on a daily basis, and it was only a matter of time until it all caught up with me. I was released from jail late that night without any bail being set and given a court date to return.

I sat on the steps outside the jail, picked up a cigarette butt lying on the ground, and smoked it. Shortly after, I saw Paul's car appear. He told me to get in.

He said, "What's going on with you?"

I offered a number of justifications as to why I was arrested and explained to him that I was not done using yet. He told me I needed help and I was on my way to an early death from overdosing. In my delusional head, I disagreed with him.

I had just left a jail cell because I had my head up my ass, but I thought I still knew all the answers. Judging by the train wreck my life was up to this point, I should have listened to him with no questions asked. But I was still resisting his recommendations.

Paul told me I needed to go to treatment, and when I said no, he told me to get out of his car. What I was really doing was running from life. I tried my best to put up this hard, external shell. I was full of fear. None of it was working.

I looked down the road, which seemed to be a never-ending street with nothing but the jail on it and said, "Fine. I'll go to treatment."

I didn't agree because I wanted to go to treatment or because I wanted to get better. I agreed so that I didn't have to walk down that long street and figure out where I was going to sleep that night.

I checked into detox.

NANCY

We were relieved that JP was in detox. Paul assured us the legal issues would be sorted out and that the most important goal was to get JP into rehab after the detox.

Joe showed a lot of wisdom when he told JP to handle his own problems. That day in jail was a turning point in our son's life. Joe's decision not to discuss that phone conversation with me was also a wise choice. My husband knew all too well I would have jumped in too soon.

Dr. Cipriano has a saying I had heard him repeat frequently over the years but had never fully grasped until then: "The readiness is all." With several hundred miles separating them—Joe standing in water flooding the floor in Rhode Island, and JP sitting in a jail cell in South Florida—*readiness* had taken hold.

Later that week, I was on the bleachers at an indoor ice rink watching Grace take a figure skating lesson when my cell phone rang. It was the therapist from the detox with a call from JP. JP and I began talking, and his mood quickly escalated into rage.

I was in a public place, but my body started shaking uncontrollably and it wasn't because the ice rink was cold. I just could not handle what was going on with him. He kept on yelling and cursing until finally the therapist intervened and ended the phone call.

I sat there afterward, struggling to regain my composure as I watched Grace glide on the ice. I was inhabiting two worlds. And I was worn.

What I did not know then was that awful phone call with JP would be the last disastrous conversation I would ever have with him. Prayers for a moment of clarity and a "spiritual awakening" were about to be answered.

JP

After a few days at detox, I had a conversation with my mother from the therapist's office. I told my mother I planned on going back to the halfway house where I had been using once I completed detox. My mother explained to me that if I did that, they were completely finished with me. But that if I went to treatment for several weeks, there was a slim chance I could earn my way back to the family.

I reacted violently. I threatened to leave rehab, I threatened physical violence against the staff members. In essence, I threw an adult temper tantrum on the phone with my mother.

Pretty pathetic.

Somewhere very far back in my mind, I heard a sober voice that I hadn't heard for a long time. The tone of the voice was calm and powerful, and it said maybe you should just do this. Maybe your way is wrong and everybody else is right. Maybe you should just give up and stop trying to win this thing.

I agreed to go to treatment.

Most of me still didn't want to get sober, but after about a week into treatment I realized that I needed to stop. I had tried everything else but what everyone told me to do. I decided I was going to give getting sober 100 percent, and if that didn't work, then I was really destined to be a failure.

Following that cluster of thoughts, I felt calm. I felt a different breath of life flow into me. I could almost feel God's hand on my back.

I was finally going to wave the white flag. But this was a different white flag. I was surrendering for my health, peace of mind, and happiness. I was no longer going to be dragged through the broken glass by my addiction.

I knew I was done.

I had been so full of shit for the longest time and had lied to everybody and said, "I am done" that I decided this time, I wasn't going to say anything. I was going to *show* them through my actions.

NANCY

During the weeks JP was doing his second stint in rehab, something changed. We didn't talk a lot, but during one phone call he told me he attended Sunday Mass. After Mass, he did not get up to leave right away. He remained seated in the pew until he was alone in the church.

"I felt the presence of God there, Mom. It was like the Adoration Chapel at home. I could feel God with me. I want to go there with you, Mom. I want to take you to that church."

I knew after so many false starts, lies, and pure BS over the years there was a better-than-average chance this story was more of the same. But something registered differently to me in my heart. I began to realize the *Secret Belief was happening.*

The reports from the professionals at the rehab were that JP truly was doing well and committed to staying sober. We hadn't seen him for ten months. They told us to come down to discuss his after-care plans. Joe was really booked with work. We decided I would go with Molly and Grace, so they could spend time with their brother as well. When the three of us arrived at the rehab, I could see there was something different about the way he carried himself. Of course, I was guarded.

But this time he got it.

We visited the church together where he had experienced the presence of God. For the record, it was on the way back from seeing his attorney—not the most pleasant of office visits. But in keeping with the script of being on a new, better path, I didn't dwell on what came immediately before the church visit.

We were in the church for just a few moments because the sexton said the building was closed. Being with JP even briefly in that church was powerful. We were alone together in a silent, sacred space. It was an assurance our family was truly on the right footing. It was time to begin the welcome to the son who had gone so far from home.

JP chose to enter a well-respected, structured after-care program once he completed treatment. Making that choice on his own indicated a lot about the positive direction he wanted to be headed. He got a job and a sponsor and went to meetings. He was following what 12-step programs call Good Orderly Direction—GOD. I guess they call it that for good reason.

Six weeks later, JP flew back to New York for Molly's high school graduation party. He was home for less than forty-eight hours, but it was amazing to see the change in him. It was the first time he had been home as a son participating in our family's life for many years. During the party, JP didn't follow his usual pattern of sitting alone on the edges of the gathering or leaving. He enjoyed talking to family and friends he hadn't seen for a long time. At one point, he went to a quiet room in the house with Marie, a dear cousin of mine, who has a healing ministry. They prayed together, and she spoke to him about his life and God's love. JP said later that his time with Marie was a powerful experience.

Before JP left the next morning to go back to Florida, Jim, Tara, and their children came over for breakfast. Our two families all packed into our kitchen together. There was a lot of laughter, and this time JP was part of that laughter. It was a wonderful way to end the weekend. While Joe took JP to the airport, Jim, Tara, and I stayed awhile in the kitchen. We all agreed a change had taken place in JP's life. He had a purposeful look in his eye.

An incredible blessing.

Chapter 25

THE STARTING BLOCK

JP

When I got out of treatment, I went to a reputable halfway house. This wasn't a lockdown type of facility. There were a few expectations that needed to be met. You had to abide by a curfew, attend a community meeting, take a drug test regularly, and get a job.

Nothing forces you to get sober. It's good to have safety nets in place along with a structured life as they are a constant force pushing back against addictive thoughts. But there are a lot of times that a halfway house, probation, job, and drug testing aren't enough to stop an addict from getting high.

However, with those safety nets in place, if that individual wants to stop, there are now more reasons to do so.

Addiction is a very tricky, insidious thing. Many distortions occur in the brain, which addicted individuals believe. But accountability and potential consequences may encourage an even slightly motivated person to get sober.

When I got out of rehab for the second time, I was that slightly motivated person. In fact, this time, I was more than slightly motivated. I was sick of feeling the way I felt. I had been a charismatic, funny, and social guy—or so I was told. But I wasn't comfortable in my skin. Every morning when I woke up, I felt like the world was ending. There was this desperate churning in my core. The unhealthy way that I had always shut that churning off was by using.

In previous half-assed attempts to change, I hung out with people who were not serious about getting sober. And I relapsed every time.

But I had decided I was absolutely not going to do that this time around.

This time around I got a job, went to 12-step meetings, and got a 12-step sponsor. I lived life in a disciplined manner. I only hung around guys who had over a year sober, I prayed, and I went straight to bed. Anything I perceived as negative or taking me from my goal of getting some sober time together, I immediately distanced myself from.

In the past, I had always prided myself on "not being a snitch." As I got sober this time, my understanding of what that really meant grew. I had to change the definition of "snitching." A snitch tells on someone else's bad behavior out of spite, jealousy, or selfishness.

While I was living in the halfway house, I was faced with a dilemma. The rules of the halfway house were that if someone was using, you were responsible for turning them in. In the past, this was something I had never done as it went against my commitment not to be a snitch.

But now things were different for me. An individual in the halfway house was using, and I didn't want to be around that. I had to do something. I realized my motives were not out of spite, jealously, or selfishness. My motive to tell the people running the halfway house that this guy was using was self-preservation—*my life was on the line.*

The thought I had about this individual and this situation was this: if you want to get high, you can go do it on the streets—not in the halfway house. I had the mindset of a football player rushing yards with his arm up. I had to stiff-arm anything that could potentially lead me to using.

So, I did.

I let the staff members know about the guy, and he was out. Dilemma solved, and my sobriety stayed intact.

There were other behaviors and things I had to change within the first few months of sobriety. I couldn't get into fights anymore—or at least it was recommended to me not to.

One night I was on a date and I was driving the girl home. I saw a guy whom I hadn't seen in months walking down the street. I stopped the car and said hello to him. I was being friendly.

He asked me if I could give him a ride up the street to the bus stop. I told him the buses weren't running at that time because it was late at night. He began to get agitated.

He said, "I know that. I'm going to pick shit up."

I then told him I wouldn't give him a ride to help him buy drugs, that he should go enjoy his night, and if he needed help to call me.

He wasn't taking no for an answer.

He began screaming: "Come on. Give me a ride, mother fucker."

This guy was now disrespecting me, and it was in front of an audience whom I wanted to impress. The option of knocking this kid's teeth down his throat was right there in my mind. I knew that physically he was not a threat to me. But I also knew fighting because I felt he disrespected me was not "the right thing to do" in my new, sober life.

I made a good choice. I told him I was going to pray for him and drove away.

I drove about two blocks and had to stop the car because I was so tempted to turn the car around and go back and fight.

Right then and there I did what my 12-step buddies had taught me to do: I called one of my sober friends to bounce this situation off him. In the back of my mind, I was hoping he would give me clearance to run this kid over.

But instead, he calmly said, "JP, you did the right thing. You know you did the right thing. Keep driving."

Of course, he was right.

But my pride, ego, and distorted thoughts about what constitutes "manly behavior," were trying to tell me otherwise.

Thank God, I kept driving. It was an important moment of making a good choice in early recovery.

Throughout this time, I went to 12-step meetings regularly. I found a fellowship that I felt comfortable in. I was continuously working with my sponsor on getting through the twelve steps. I called sober guys about everything: the right way to tie my shoes, button my shirt, and wipe my ass because I now realized that I didn't know what the hell I was doing, and with a year or more sober, they obviously did. None of the suggestions or recommendations they gave me were overly difficult to follow, and after a few months of doing these things, I began to have new habits—healthy, sober habits.

What prompted me to do these things and to vigorously fight for a recovery was that I was desperate. A story in a well-known 12-step book speaks of a drowning man who was getting sucked down by thrashing waves. He reached out to grab what appeared to be a flimsy reed. That reed ultimately provided a way for him to escape the turbulent water—and it turned out to be the powerful hand of God.

I was desperate. I was scared for my life and knew that if I picked up drugs again, it was done. I wasn't even sure if all this shit was going to work, but I didn't have any other options—aside from getting a lobotomy.

Over those months, when I would see people who hadn't seen me since I was using, they would say things like, "You look so good. You seem so happy."

Before I got sober, they would say things like: "Oh my God; you are so skinny! Are you ok? Have you been sleeping?" And "Check his pulse."

Other people were seeing the change in me before I had even come to realize it. I finished the six-month commitment I had promised my family at the halfway house. I started to think, "I got this thing. I now know all the answers."

I was wrong.

I called my family, whom I was beginning to mend some of my wreckage with, and told them I was ready to get an apartment. My family, along with everybody around me, was telling me this was a very bad idea.

I didn't understand why.

The recommendation I was given was to move into a three-quarter sober living home. I thought this was a waste of time and didn't see how it would benefit me. Against my "better" thinking, I obliged. This three-quarter house had two rules: don't get high and don't get anyone else high. There was no curfew and there were no rules against having female guests. You were basically expected to do everything you had been doing—as in being a productive member of society.

Within two weeks of going to there, I had quit my job, was going out to clubs, and was sleeping through most of the day. One day I was lying on the couch feeling sorry for myself. A dear sober friend of mine, who was managing the house at the time, walked in and said, "What's up with you, man?"

I told him I wasn't sure, but I felt like I wanted to drink. I told him I wasn't happy, and I felt like everything was falling apart.

"Hey, look at what the hell you are doing," he said. "You are going out all night. You are not working. If that's what you want to do, you are well on your way back out."

He recommended that I get a job again, pick up on my meeting attendance, and reduce some of my nightly activities.

I wised up and took his advice.

The old me would have felt sorry for myself or been tempted to get high. The difference now was that I was willing. I was willing to change and willing to take suggestions from other sober men, in addition to tapping into a wealth of spirituality through prayer and meditation as recommended in 12-step programs.

This previously untapped resource of prayer and meditation was an important part of my recovery. Don't get me wrong. I didn't go out and shave my head and walk around in a cloak like a monk or join the seminary, but I was certainly open to deepening some sort of spiritual connection because that is an essential part of getting and staying sober.

Once I took these suggestions, life got back on the right track within a matter of days.

At seven months sober, I decided to begin schooling to become a clinician and earn my CASAC certification (Certified Alcohol and Substance Abuse Counselor). From a young age, with no foreshadowing of the struggles that I would endure, I had wanted to be a therapist. At eight months sober, with the help of a friend, I was able to get a job at a rehab. I started at the place as a night shift technician. I was then asked to manage a halfway house. The things that were happening inwardly and outwardly to me were astonishing.

If you had taken me like the Ghost of Christmas Future

and showed me how I felt and where my life would be at eight months sober, I would not have ever believed you. I began sponsoring guys. Things just kept getting better in all aspects.

Mind you, I still struggled from time to time. But I was easily able to manage any bullshit rumblings my suppressed addiction would throw my way. I successfully completed all twelve steps, which is similar to being a Marine. Once you are a Marine, you're always a Marine. Once you're an alcoholic and admit that to yourself, you continuously work the twelve steps throughout your daily life.

On April 6, 2011, I celebrated one year sober. This did not seem real to me. I kept thinking there had to be one day over the past year that I used. But there wasn't. Passing the one-year threshold of sobriety was a bigger rush than any of the bullshit I had previously used.

My family flew down, and I had a big party for my one year. Things continued to improve, and I continued to gain momentum in life.

After my family went back to New York, just a few days after celebrating my one year with them, I had severe pain in my mouth. I had to have emergency surgery with three impacted wisdom teeth extracted, which was a complicated procedure.

Before the procedure I told the oral surgeon that I was in recovery and did not want any narcotic medication. He told me that due to the nature of the procedure, this was not an option, but he would give me the lowest acceptable dosage.

Afterward, I was in immense pain. With the supervision of my sober support network, I took three doses of the prescribed pain medication. I didn't really feel high and didn't even like the way it felt anymore. The next day I got up and disposed of the remaining prescription.

I then had to go to the class I was taking to get my clinician's license. I could sense on the drive to school that something was off with me. For the past year, I had not been the angry or extremely agitated person I once was. But for some reason, that anger and agitation had resurfaced.

I sat in class for about twenty minutes and did not like

what was being discussed. I grabbed my book bag and stormed out of class. On my way back to my car, I passed an individual in the stairwell. I felt like he was walking too close to me, and I leaned into his face as I passed him.

He looked at me like I was crazy.

When I got to my car, I thought to myself, "What the hell is going on? You haven't done shit like that in over a year."

What was happening was that—regardless of it being pre-scribed, not abused, well-supervised, and barely taken—the medication had awakened the monster. I remember thinking that everything in my life was a lie, that I hadn't accomplished anything. I remember wanting to fight someone.

I reached out for help to a sober friend and was told to get my ass to a meeting and double up on everything: meetings, prayer, and phone calls to sober friends. Within a few days of doing that, everything was back in order.

In addition to the counseling classes I was taking, I began college classes, which were challenging and reward-ing. At this point in time, I had already received my high school diploma. I enrolled in a weekend college program four hours away, on the west coast of Florida, so that I could keep my full-time job and go to school full time as well. Every month I would leave on Thursday, drive across Florida, and attend forty hours of classes from Thursday night until Sunday evening. I would then head back across the state for another four-hour drive and be at work Mon-day morning. It took me four-and-a-half years to earn my college degree.

I continued to work at rehab for the next year and a half and was promoted to shift supervisor. I worked my ass off. But I had the desire to succeed.

Relationships with my family and friends were growing strong and continuously gaining momentum.

NANCY

Joe and I believed that God had touched our son powerfully and was guiding him. Watching him, month by month, work so hard to go to school and continue to be promoted at his job was one of the greatest experiences of our lives.

JP would call us during those long rides to and from school. It was a good time to catch up on what he was doing. As he would drive home Sunday night, he would call oftentimes just to help him stay awake. Joe and I felt profound gratitude for the miracle of recovery in JP's life and for all his efforts day after day after day to sustain that miracle.

The twelve steps are a bond I love having with my son. One of the most memorable experiences JP and I have shared was visiting Stepping Stones, the home of AA's co-founder Bill W., and his wife, Lois. Stepping Stones in Bedford Hills, New York, is listed on the National Register of Historic places, and it is where Bill W. wrote many of his books and where Lois founded the Al-Anon movement for families. Thousands of people from all over the world go to visit. For many, visiting Stepping Stones is a spiritual pilgrimage affirming their commitment to a sober life.

Over the years, I have read many books about Bill W. and Dr. Bob, their amazing friendship and the history of the founding of AA. I had seen black-and-white photos of Bill W. in his house. Stepping Stones is within driving distance from our home, and I wanted to go there with JP. A small window of time opened for us during a visit in early summer after he celebrated two years sober. On the way, we stopped at his favorite place for barbeque ribs. We sat at a small table outside and talked about what he was doing in Florida with work and school. As always, he had me laughing with his stories about the people he encountered. JP can read people's motives with laser insight, and when he tells stories, his imitations of people are not only very humorous but they nail the truths of that person's character.

Stepping Stones is tucked away at the end of a very quiet street. JP stepped out of the car and stood silently for a few minutes.

"I can just *feel* it, Mom. I can just feel the power here."

I sensed it too. It may sound a little *out there* as in "May the Force be with you," but as others have described places of pilgrimage and faith, there was a presence and peacefulness at Stepping Stones.

I have a well-earned reputation in my family as being incredibly clumsy, so when JP saw that some of the paths were uneven, he gently took my arm to help guide me around without a mishap. We walked to the unassuming cinderblock building on the knoll where Bill W. wrote books that have been read by millions. We said very little as we walked the paths together.

The house where Bill W. and Lois lived was closed that day, but we were able to sit on the screened-in porch overlooking the property. On the porch, there were old black-and-white photos of the early members of AA sitting on the very furniture we were sitting on.

JP and I sat together in silence, taking it all in. As we headed back to the car, JP walked a bit, then stopped, and for a good amount of time stood alone looking out over the woods. The only sound was that of birds singing. The sunlight through the trees made a dappled brightness that surrounded him. It was all incredibly green and beautiful.

I wanted to take a picture of that moment, but I didn't want anything to disturb it. My son had come so far—he had recovered his intelligence, his faith, his kindness, his sense of humor, and his humanity. I felt a huge measure of gratitude for his life, for his choice to be in recovery, and for the gift of sharing that with him.

I also felt a desire to want to reshape time, to get back what we had lost and extend out even longer the time we had together.

That's the mother in me, I guess.

After a while JP walked back over to me and took my hand.

"This was beautiful, JP. This is something I will always cherish. It meant everything to me, Manz."

"I know, Ma. Me too. This place is really special. I am glad we came."

Chapter 26

CHALLENGES

JP

Throughout my childhood one of my biggest fears was that something would happen to my parents. During my stints of short-term sobriety and now long-term sobriety, this fear grew. I was afraid of harm, or even worse, happening to them.

But the fact is that in sobriety you learn to walk through fear.

The summer I was four years sober, I was given the opportunity to spend the month of July in Rhode Island with my family before I started a new job as a counselor at a treatment program in South Florida. I had an incredible time. During that month, it was really great being able to spend all that time with my parents, sisters, and Goggy, my grandmother, doing the things we love to do. We went out on the boat and to the beach together. My dad and I went out for dinner in New York. My mom, my sister, Grace, and I visited Newport.

There's a spot where you can sit on a high point overlooking Newport Harbor where Bill W. sat with his wife, Lois, just before he was shipped off to fight in World War I. He had experienced the presence of God there, which he wrote about. The three of us went to that spot at dusk one night together. We took the whole thing in, and we prayed there, too. It was pretty amazing.

When it was time to leave, my dad offered to keep me company and help with the driving for half the way back down to Florida. We went as far as Charleston, South Carolina, together. My dad drove my Camaro, and it was a good time. We stopped at a barbeque place together. We listened to each other's music. My dad didn't know I liked so many of the songs from his generation. We sang the lyrics of the songs together as we drove south.

I got back to Florida ready to start my new job. About a week later, we received the news that my father was diagnosed with cancer and had to have surgery. This was devastating. One of my greatest fears had horribly happened.

I jumped on a plane to New York and was there for the surgery and for the days afterward when he was in the hospital. This was one of the most difficult things I have ever had to endure: watching the person who is hands-down the strongest, most hardworking and altruistic man I know feel in pain, helpless, and scared. I was there for my family, and we all got through it together.

I often question my core values and my character. I always see my flaws a lot quicker than I see my strengths. But when you are put into a trying situation like that, your true colors will show. Everyone was scared, but as a family we all tightened up, took care of my dad, covered each other's backs, and faced the fear together.

Thank God, my father recovered from the surgery. I got back on a flight and went back to work at my new job in Florida.

NANCY

We were having a wonderful summer. A few days after Joe returned from *The Great American Father & Son Road Trip*, he went for a routine test. And just that fast, our world was upended.

Ten days later, on the morning of Joe's surgery, Annie, JP, and Molly accompanied us to the hospital. Grace stayed home with close family friends, as we knew it would be a very long day. Right after we got to the waiting room, Annie's friend Kelly, who sees Joe as a second father, showed up unannounced, carrying large bags filled with junk food, water bottles, coffee, and newspapers. While this may sound a little irreverent, the six of us passed the hours of waiting for Joe to come out of the surgery, telling stories about things that happened when they were all growing up together in our parish grammar school. JP did his spot-on imitations of old teachers, family friends, school cronies, and me in my more (ahem) high-decibel parenting moments that made us all laugh—probably too loudly—in the waiting room. Later in the day, Joe's brother Bob arrived. I was so thankful they all were there.

When Joe came out of the surgery, we crowded around his bed in the recovery room. Even with an oxygen mask and all kinds of tubes and monitors on, Joe put us at ease with his humor, asking us to get him a Taco Bell beef burrito.

After all the years of questioning the soundness of our family and feeling so beat up by the circumstances of JP's life—as he calls it, "back in the day"—I quickly realized a greater truth about all of us through Joe's illness: we were always committed to staying strong and riding out the challenges life poses as best as we possibly could *together as a family*.

Over the years, I learned that life offers gifts in the midst of darkness. These gifts can be recognized and appreciated because you develop some kind of *stealth dark-night-of-the-soul vision powers* that you just don't have when everything is all sunshine and lollipops. JP's addiction and recovery initiated me into the terrible beauty you can see with those nocturnal vision powers usually possessed only by some feral night creature. Joe's illness honed to a fine point my ability to see the gifts born of a dark season. Again, the situation is nothing I would ever ask God for, but it is ultimately how God worked in our lives.

I came to trust that my family could count on one another no matter what. I came to believe that all the hopeless lies about our family that ate at my soul like acid during the years we battled against addiction—that we were grossly flawed and sentenced to an existence of struggle and failure—were complete bullshit thrown out by the one St. Ignatius of Loyola calls "the enemy."

Our family's Round II with facing down a life-threatening challenge cemented in my soul the lessons I learned in Round I with JP's illness of addiciton: we are stronger for the struggle, and the very place that seemed to be our point of weakness was in fact the place where strength would take root and flourish. My beloved friend Tina has always said that when a bone is broken, it heals twice as strong in the place where the fracture occurs. A day at a time, with God's grace, we live Tina's wise words.

JP

Two weeks after my dad's surgery, we received the news that he was going to have to go through chemotherapy. When my mother called to tell me this, any warmth or security I was feeling about life quickly became frigid. The fear kicked me in the stomach like a donkey on steroids. Whatever small plans or ideas I had for that day were blasted out of my mind.

I didn't know what to expect or what was coming down the road. And it seemed like no one did. That just intensified the raw and rough emotions tied to the situation.

I thought to myself, "I have to get up there. I have to be with them."

Within a few weeks, I walked away from my life in Florida, packed up, and drove up to New York. I started a new job and was with my family and gave them my support throughout the months of my father's chemo treatments.

I didn't allow the thought of anything bad happening to my dad ever to enter my mind. After six long months, my father completed the treatments and is healthy and cancer free to date.

The fact is that as a family, we all trusted God, continued to walk through the fear, and supported one another. As a result, our family has grown stronger from this. There is a quote I can identify with: "You'll never know how strong you are, until being strong is your only option."

NANCY

Joe met the challenge of chemotherapy with the same quiet determination and strength that has molded his being since he was a young man. His first chemo treatment was on a cold, rainy Friday afternoon at the end of September. Annie and Molly came to the hospital with us. JP was in Florida finishing the last class for his bachelor's degree and checked in by phone throughout the day. He called again on Saturday night.

"I'm coming home," he announced. "I've thought about it. I've prayed about it. I've made up my mind. I'm moving back to New York. I want to be with Dad and all of you while you are going through this."

We told him that was a crazy idea—he had just started a new job.

"No, my mind is made up. I will be driving up Thanksgiving weekend, and I will find an apartment and work from New York. It is all arranged. And I am not changing my mind."

We tried, but there was no talking JP out of his decision. He had to take a pretty sizable pay cut for the job he would be doing in New York, and he had already applied for a master's program in counseling in Florida. But pretty quickly we realized it was a done deal, and we began to trust he was making the right decision.

It was a tremendous comfort to have him home. On chemo days, Annie, Molly, and JP would rearrange their work and school commitments to come to the hospital. Joe's days there were about ten hours long, so their presence really helped pass the time. It almost felt like we were all in our family room together—talking, laughing, watching TV, or working on our computers. Sometimes Joe would take a nap. Those times together with Joe were one of the most profound gifts that came under the heading of dark gifts.

But a gift nevertheless.

That winter my mother, who had been living in our converted barn for seven years, was in the final stages of the fight she had been bravely waging for more than a decade against a degenerative neurological disease. She was prey to infections from sepsis, requiring prolonged stays in the ICU. Unfortunately, every three weeks when Joe had a short "break" from chemo were the very times she became ill. At times that winter, our family life felt like an endurance test:

trying to help Joe as he became increasingly weak from chemo treatments and my mother as she fought a losing battle against her own failing body.

Late in January, a blizzard engulfed the East Coast. When I went in to do my daily morning check on my mother, I found her barely breathing and collapsed in a heap on the floor. I ran over to get the kids to help. Even Joe, who was not supposed to be outside because a side effect of the chemo was a dangerous sensitivity to cold, went to help.

With the ambulance on the way, we realized the snow was too deep for it to get up our long, steep driveway. The kids were still in their pajamas, shoveling as fast as possible. JP had gotten up so quickly he was outside in pajama bottoms without a coat or shirt on. I remember seeing him shirtless in the cold pushing the snow blower with heavy snow swirling around, trying to make a path for the gurney to get up to my mom. Thankfully, she got to the hospital and received the urgent care she needed.

Throughout Joe's six months of chemo, JP made a habit of having lunch with me when his work schedule permitted. It was always great to hear his voice on the phone.

"Hey, Mom, what are you doing in twenty minutes? Let's grab some lunch at the Café."

I treasured those lunches together. For many years, we never shared a lot of milestones that mothers and sons share together. But that winter we did regain lost time. It was a different context, but a regaining nonetheless.

I would be lying if I did not say there were times during those months and afterward when I felt anxious and afraid for what the future might hold. My fearful thoughts are a dangerous neighborhood to be in—make that a *very dangerous* neighborhood. I counted JP among those who stuck close and helped me keep on course as I saw Joe increasingly worn down and my mother deteriorating.

JP would firmly tell me God was taking care of all of us. A core principle of 12-step programs is Step Three: "Made a decision to turn our will and our lives over to the care of God as we understood Him." We both knew that in whatever challenges life poses, we shared a belief in a caring God to help us no matter what. JP's presence that winter just helped make that belief a little easier to hold onto.

Joe took his last chemo pill at home on his birthday on March 10. Weeks before, our kids planned a special birthday/end-of-chemo celebration at a steakhouse. Uncle Bob was invited, of course, but we kept that a secret from Joe. It was a great surprise for him when we arrived at the restaurant and Uncle Bob was waiting in the lobby. There were lots of bear hugs and joy that we all were together for a double celebration in his honor.

During dinner each one of us made a toast to Joe. When JP spoke, his voice was uncharacteristically soft, and he had to stop several times because he was fighting back tears.

"Dad, you are most courageous man I know. You are the strongest man I know. *You carried us*—all of us—through the chemo, Dad. Not the other way around. It was you carrying us.

"Your strength was the example to all of us. We leaned on you.

"You are my role model, Dad. You worked every day. You never stopped doing what you had to do for our family. You never complained. Not once. You made us laugh. You are always there for all of us. You have never stopped being there for all of us, no matter what.

"If I could be half the man you are, Daddy . . . if I could live up to half of your example. You are my hero, Dad. I love you."

Chapter 27

HOMECOMING

NANCY

When Joe's treatment was completed with a clean bill of health, JP moved back to Florida to resume his life there. As much as I wanted him to stay, I knew that was what he had to do. Years before, I never could have foreseen our son's strength and accompaniment through one of the most difficult times of our family's life. It was God's richly imaged promise in the Old Testament coming to fruition:

"I will repay you for the years the locust has eaten—the great locust and the young locust, the other locusts and the locust swarm—my great army that I sent among you." (Jl 2:25)

While he was in Florida, we spoke often on the phone. During one conversation, I told him how badly I felt about everything that had taken place during those years.

"I can't stand that it all happened the way it did, JP. I wish it could have been easier. I wish it hadn't been so painful and difficult. It was so grimy at times. Why couldn't it have just been simple?"

"Mom, I've thought about that a lot and I realized it took what it took. This was what I had to go through to be where I am today. All of it had to happen, just the way it happened. And if it hadn't, I wouldn't be the person I am now, doing what I do now.

"It was part of God's plan that way, Mom. It was what I had to go through."

That day, JP's words penetrated my heart. For the first time, it made sense. The *Secret Belief* was no longer a secret. That day I realized I needed to stop living as if I was wearing a big scarlet letter *S* for shame on my shirt, mourning the way things went into a crash-and-burn and the fact that my cherished plans for how my teenage son's life would unfold blew up in my face.

It happened as it was supposed to happen to bring us all to a place of greater understanding with a tremendous fund of shared love and commitment to service.

A year later, JP accepted an offer to open and co-own a new treatment facility in Massachusetts. The location of the new job meant he would be living an easy drive from our home and we could get together more often without the hassle of plane trips.

JP

In 2015, I was given the opportunity to form a partnership with a friend to open Northeast Addictions Treatment Center in Quincy, Massachusetts. I was able to couple my experience and training and integrate it into a program in an attempt to save lives. We have been incredibly successful in battling the opioid and drug epidemic and improving the mental health and quality of life of those we serve. We have experienced massive strategic growth at Northeast Addictions Treatment Center.

People often say when someone becomes a minister or a teacher that it's a calling. I never really understood that and thought people only worked for money. But I started to understand it when I began to work in the substance abuse treatment field. I have always felt a calling to serve those afflicted with what I struggled with. By opening Northeast, I was given the opportunity to do so. If you asked me eight years ago if I thought I would be one of the owners of a treatment center, and be given an opportunity to help all those who came in, I wouldn't have believed you.

In my work to help those struggling with addiction, I like working hard with the sickest clients because that was me.

When I meet with a client, it's almost like it's not even me speaking. The right things that need to be said kind of just flow out of my mouth. It's like I'm on autopilot.

I think because of how I was, it's easy for me to encounter and meet difficult clients exactly where they are, in whatever circumstances they are in. If you put someone who isn't sure or fairly opposed to getting sober in front of me, nine times out of ten I can convince that person it's a good idea to seek help. I see it as a challenge and almost a twisted game of mental chess.

Mind you, the individual still must do a lot of work to obtain and maintain sobriety. I know that, for me, speaking with someone who had tattoos or was close in age to me impacted me more.

The disease of alcoholism and drug addiction is like a scary, insidious dream, but you can wake up from it. Sometimes you need someone to shake you, so you can open your eyes.

That's what was done for me.

I will make sure I am continuously around to do that for others.

NANCY

We are deeply blessed to be a family that has been restored. That does not mean we are perfect—far from it. We all have our flaws and moments of disagreement. But our core is strong love and a sense of loyalty to one another, born from our commitment to stand together even when the going gets *very* tough.

On a pretty regular basis, the phone rings and the voice on the other end is a parent seeking help for an adult child who is making addiction-fueled choices that are causing chaos and misery for the addict and everyone else.

These parents have heard from a friend of a friend about the turnaround in JP's life and ours. They always have a lot of questions about how it took place and what they need to do to make it happen. I can always hear the fear in their voices because by the time they call, things have gone pretty far downhill.

Coupled with that fear is also a flicker of hope that they too will see their beloved son or daughter grab hold of a new way of life and survive. Whenever these calls come in, they are an immediate priority. When the conversation ends, I always try to stop and reflect on the family's needs. And in that pause, I always feel a powerful outpouring of gratitude in my heart for how it all worked out for us. The gratitude leads me to pray for that family's moment of homecoming.

If I could capture an image of our family's homecoming, it would be what I saw at our recent Fourth of July party in Rhode Island. The Fourth of July is a big deal for our family—well I guess it's fair to say we love to celebrate all holidays. On that day, our house was filled with lots of family and friends, lots of food, and lots of laughter.

For just a moment, I stepped back from the busyness of getting out food for a hungry crowd of twenty-five and saw an answer to desperate prayers from years before. Sitting in a circle of white chairs on our lawn overlooking the pond, enjoying a red, white, and blue beauty of a day, were Joe, JP, Jim, Tara, Paul, Molly, JP's fiancé Jess, and JP's business partner Rich and his wife, Lee. Across the yard Grace, her cousins, and family friends were playing a lively game of Heads Up.

The homecoming was right before my eyes.

Homecoming implies that a *home leaving* has taken place. For some families, it's as simple as packing up the car with suitcases and dropping their son off at summer camp, or college, or a trip backpacking through Europe. That's the pretty straightforward rite of passage many young adults and their families make. For JP, the journey of home leaving was a wrenching experience that took us all to a razor's edge.

In Luke's gospel, the Prodigal Son, through the grace of God, has his moment of *metanoia*, the Greek word meaning *conversion of heart*. The son—who chose insult, self-exile, and a life of dissolution—realizes his destiny was not to be scrounging with pigs for food. He experiences a moment of clarity and heads home to be welcomed back by his father, who has been watching and waiting. In our family's story,

God's grace brought that *metanoia moment* to JP's heart, leading to his homecoming and, ultimately, a path of service to others through the wisdom accrued on his own journey.

All the paths—however twisted and rubble strewn—brought us to that gorgeous July day. When the food was ready, the twenty-five of us gathered in a circle around the picnic table for Joe to lead us in a blessing.

It does not get any better than that.

Everyone stood there for a moment after Joe's prayer, and for one split second, the final lines of a poem by Robert Louis Stevenson flashed through my mind like a benediction:

> *"Home is the sailor, home from the sea,*
> *And the hunter home from the hill."*[5]

Our very foundation had been sorely tried. But now we were all home together. As a family, we have endured, our commitment to each other strengthened through the loving constancy of God.

Do I hear an Amen?

---

5   Robert Louis Stevenson, "Requiem. "Public domain.

ABOUT THE AUTHORS

Nancy McCann Vericker is a spiritual director, youth minister, and retreat speaker. She holds a master's degree in spiritual direction from Fordham University. She has worked as parish coordinator of family faith-building programs and teaches a Bible study for women in her parish. She and her husband, Joe, a professional photographer, have been married since 1983. The couple has four children and lives in Westchester County, New York.

www.nancyvericker.com

JP Vericker is co-founder of Northeast Addictions Treatment Center in Massachusetts. He is board certified in the treatment of addictions. He began his work in the substance abuse treatment field as a night shift technician and has worked his way up in his career through a variety of positions including halfway house manager, detox counselor, detox manager, marketing consultant, licensing consultant, and therapist. He lives in Massachusetts.

Made in the USA
Middletown, DE
28 August 2018